GENERATIONS
SHOULD
REMEMBER

Bohdan Rymaszewski

GENERATIONS
SHOULD
REMEMBER

Auschwitz-Birkenau State Museum, Oświęcim 2003

First published in Polish in 2000 under the title:
Pamiętać będą pokolenia

Translation:
Letterman Sp. z o.o.
Agencja tłumaczy, Kraków

English edition prepared by:
Marilyn Kupetz

Cover:
Piotr Kutryba, Wiesław Zieliński

Consultation:
Jolanta Adamska, Jacek Nowakowski, Franciszek Piper,
Teresa Świebocka, Jerzy Wróblewski, Wiesław Wysocki

Photograps:
Archives of the Auschwitz-Birkenau State Museum, Oświęcim
Bohdan Rymaszewski, Lidia Foryciarz

The publication of this book was funded by the Foundation for the
Commemoration of the Victims of Auschwitz-Birkenau Death Camp

ISBN 83-88526-33-2

Printed by Cieszyńska Drukarnia Wydawnicza, Cieszyn ul. Pokoju Poland

Table of Contents

Preface – *Jerzy Wróblewski* 7
Introduction 13
The Estabilishmet, Development, and Inmates of Auschwitz . 19
Auschwitz II-Birkenau: The Primary Site for the Extermination
    of European Jewry 33
On Both Sides of the Gate Inscribed Arbeit macht frei . . . 41
After the Liberation of the Camp 57
Cemetery 67
Historical Monument and Monument 75
Museum 99
A Place of Remembrance 105
Continuing Reflections of Auschwitz 113
Epilogue 133
Bibliography 135

Preface

The Auschwitz-Birkenau State Museum, in Oświęcim, Poland, and the Foundation for Remembrance of the Victims of the Death Camp at Auschwitz-Birkenau proudly presents Generations Should Remember, Dr. Bohdan Rymaszewski's sensitive, authoritative account of the preservation of the Auschwitz concentration camp and its evidence.

Unfortunately, very little has been written about the conservation and protection of what remains of the former camp. Most writers have been concerned with documenting the crimes, with the numbers and origins of the prisoners and the ways of commemorating them, as well as with the symbolism of Auschwitz and the education of the young, post-Auschwitz generations. The relatively few works written about conservation issues remain somewhere on the periphery.

Rymaszewski's account is a welcome addition to the literature. For many years, Rymaszewski has been interested in the preservation of the material heritage of Auschwitz, and he has been involved in important decisions concerning its conservation. He gives advice, helps, and teaches.

Any conversation about the preservation of Auschwitz begins with the former prisoners of the camp. After the end of the war, many prisoners carefully tried to limit destruction of what remained, largely to document the crimes that had been committed there. Thanks to their initiative, on July 2, 1947, the Polish Parliament passed a law imposing an obligation to protect "forever" the area of the former camp as well as all the extant buildings and furnishings. As a result, a vast, historic complex has been preserved to the present day.

The complex covers an area of almost 200 hectares and includes 154 buildings; more than 300 historic ruins, including those of the crematoria and gas chambers; and kilometers of roads and fences. Thousands of other objects have also been preserved: human hair, shoes, suitcases, and clothes. The preservation of this invaluable evidence was possible thanks to the understanding of its significance by subsequent generations of Poles.

From the beginning of the museum's existence, all the conservation work carried out in the former camp has been financed exclusively from Polish funds. The funds allocated for this purpose by the Polish Ministry of Culture and Art came from the national budget, despite other, arguably more urgent demands for subsidies. This support and commitment is important.

The government subsidies were relatively large considering Poland's postwar financial situation. Nonetheless, they proved insufficient to cover the immense amount of work in such a large complex. Critics pointed out delays in conservation and dangers threatening the camp. Others suggested that the efforts undertaken to obtain additional funding were inadequate.

Indeed, not until the late 1980s and early 1990s was it possible for the representatives of the Ronald S. Lauder's Foundation, from the United States, to work effectively with Polish experts. Together with these experts, including Ryma-szewski, they prepared a report presenting the scale of the *financial needs connected with conserving the buildings in the former camp. According to their estimates, the necessary amount was U.S.$42.5 million.*

An indispensable fundraiser was Kalman Sultanik, the future vice chairman of the International Auschwitz Council and president of the Financial Committee of that Council. The effects of his efforts were visible almost immediately.

Funding allocated by several European countries made it possible to complete the various conservation and investment tasks necessary for preserving the existing historic sites. Among the most vital:

• *installing an air-conditioning system in the most important buildings*

• *purchasing equipment for the pressure treatment of wood*

• *overhauling several dozen brick and wooden barracks, wooden watch-towers, and entrance gates*

• *exposing the foundations and remains of the wooden barracks in Birkenau*

• *replacing the pipe network for drinking water and fire--protection water*

• *introducing fire-protection installations in all the buildings of the Auschwitz Museum*

• *purchasing fire-protection equipment and vehicles for the conservator's division*

• *overhauling the "Sauna" building in Birkenau and establishing a permanent exhibition there*

• *commencing an immense and costly project, namely the repair of the original fence of the Auschwitz-Birkenau camp and many, many other works of equal importance*

The museum's only recourse was an extensive subsidy, which came from the governments of Austria, Belgium, France, Greece, Holland, Luxemburg. The German Federal Republic and individual German lands belonging to the Federation, Norway, Switzerland, and Russia. The museum also received financial support from the Foundation for Polish-German Cooperation and the Foundation for Remembrance of the Victims of the Death Camp at Auschwitz-Birkenau. The latter was established in 1990 with the purpose of gathering social funds for supporting the activity of the museum and its conservation works, research, publishing, and educational activities. The Foundation's help is extremely valuable to the museum, which is now financed mostly from the Polish national budget.

The museum is also greatly indebted to the Conservation Committee of the International Museum Council and to its presidents: Bohdan Rymaszewski and Władysław Niessner. The expert help of the eminent Polish and foreign specialists in selecting the most important tasks, methods, technologies, and conservation approaches has been invaluable and has contributed to saving many precious historic buildings.

Public support of the museum's activities and conservation efforts has been important, enduring, and greatly appreciated. Moral and financial support from Polish and foreign foundations, institutions, social organizations, and individuals testifies to the growing interest in the history of Auschwitz and to a strong desire to preserve the former camp and its artifacts so that they serve as a warning for future generations.

In 1979, when Auschwitz was included in the World Heritage List, UNESCO recognized it as a symbol and testimony of an unprecedented crime committed against the people of various nationalities. Interest in its maintenance and conservation is only natural on the part of Poles and the international community—hence the need for and value of this book. Ryma-szewski presents the history of Auschwitz, perspective on the problems posed by its conservation in general and by preserving the material relics of the camp specifically, as well as the current needs of a place that generations should remember.

Jerzy Wróblewski

Jerzy Wróblewski is director of the Auschwitz-Birkenau State Museum in Oświęcim, Poland, and chairman of the Board of the Foundation for Remembrance of the Victims of the Death Camp at Auschwitz-Birkenau.

Auschwitz I. Fragment of camp fence.

Introduction

Some events, and the places connected with them, cannot be erased by the passage of time. Passing years and changing times merely endow them with new significance. Such terrible events as genocide are not deleted from the memory of subsequent generations; rather, they reverberate in it with a dreadful echo that is also a warning.

The events that took place near the Polish town of Oświęcim, in the years 1940-1945, inflicted a painful wound on the civilized world. During World War II, when, together with the rest of Poland, the town was incorporated by the Nazis into the German Reich, an unprecedented death camp was established in its vicinity. About 1.5 million people from all over Nazi-occupied Europe, the majority of whom were Jewish, were murdered there. Also killed in the camp were some 70,000 Poles, 20,000 Gypsies, 15,000 Soviet prisoners, as well as thousands of prisoners of several dozen other nationalities.

During the period of German occupation, the German name *Auschwitz* (currently also used in many other languages) was imposed by the Nazis on Oświęcim, which had been known under this Polish name since the Middle Ages. Since the World War II, the town has been identified with the concentration camp and a place of mass death. Indeed, for no blame of its own, it is burdened with infamy. This, unfortunately, overshadows both the present daily life of the town and its respectable existence in the previous centuries. Clearly, a distinction has to be made between the Polish town of Oświęcim and Auschwitz, the former Nazi concentration camp. More than a half century ago the unprecedented death factory ceased its operation of murder of innocent people and the following questions still remain unanswered.

What Is the Present Meaning of the Heritage of Auschwitz? What Should it Be in the Future?

Any answer to these questions must take into account that the preserved buildings and equipment in the former Nazi camp are to a greater or lesser extent related to the town, to numerous nearby villages, to the fragments of the communication network, as well as to the nearby factories and other enterprises. The former camp itself, on the other hand, has now many diverse functions that are sometimes contradictory: It is a cemetery, a historic monument, a museum, and a place of remembrance.

These functions lead to contradictory demands, and the only way to solve these problems involves compromises that take into account the sensitivities of the interested parties. The basic dilemma is expressed in the following question: How can the remnants of Auschwitz be protected as a document of the past without interfering with normal, contemporary life in Oświęcim and other towns nearby?

This publication aims to answer this question to some extent. It does not offer a single, final response because the passing of time and changing conditions have led to some

Auschwitz I. Fragment of double rows of electrified barbed wire fence.

permanent modifications. However, the underlying principle should always be faithful dedication to the memory of everything that Auschwitz symbolizes.

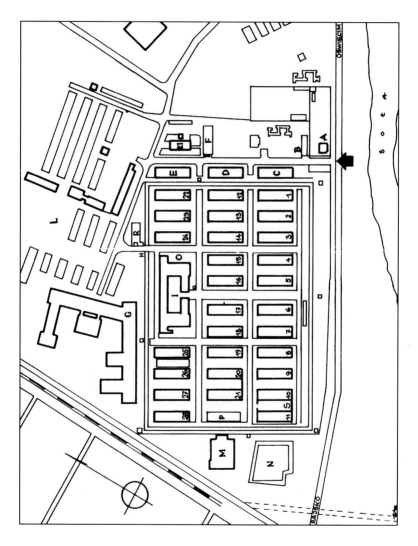

Plan of Auschwitz I, by Tadeusz Kinowski.

Auschwitz I.

A	House of camp commander.
B	Main guardhouse.
C	Camp headquarters.
D	Camp administration offices.
E	SS hospital.
F	Political division office (camp Gestapo).
G	Camp admissions building.
H	Main gate with the inscription "Arbeit macht frei."
I	Kitchen.
KI	Gas chamber and Crematorium I.
L	Farm buildings and workshops.
M	Warehouse with items confiscated from murdered inmates.
N	Gravel pit (place of executions).
O	Place where camp orchestra played.
P	Laundry facilities.
R	Guardhouse of block managers.
S	Execution wall
1-28	Prisoners' blocks.

Auschwitz I and some contemporary development in the town of Oświęcim. Aerial view.

Photo: W. Gorgolewski 1996

The Establishment, Development, and Inmates of Auschwitz

The project of creating a concentration camp in the District of Katowice (which encompasses the town of Oświęcim) was conceived at the end of 1939, in the office of the senior SS and police commander in Wrocław. At that time, the office was presided over by an SS general, Erich von dem Bach-Zelewski[1], whose name later acquired notoriety because during the Warsaw Uprising of 1944, the German troops under his command murdered thousands of Polish civilians. Some of those who survived were randomly selected and sent to the Auschwitz camp, which at that time was already operating at its full capacity.

The direct author of the idea of organizing a camp in Oświęcim, in the area of the former army barracks, was General Bach-Zelewski's subordinate, SS-Oberführer (brigadier)

---

[1] Erich von dem Bach-Zelewski was a member of the NSDAP from 1930, and, from 1933, a high-ranking SS general who held various important positions in that unit. Among others, he was the commander of the Nazi Security Service and of the Police in Wrocław. As a result of his effort, Auschwitz was established in the area under his control. From 1942, he was a plenipotentiary responsible for working against the underground armies in occupied Europe. From 1944, he commanded the corps involved in suppressing the Warsaw Uprising (August 1-October 2, 1944), and he carried out numerous actions against Polish civilians in Warsaw. After the war, he was tried by a court in the German Federal Republic for the murders committed in 1933, but he was never held formally responsible for the crimes of genocide that he had committed.

Arpad Wigand[2], an inspector of the German *Sicherheitspolizei und Sicherheitsdienst* (Sipo und SD – namely, the security police and the security service) in Silesia. He argued that the places of confinement currently established in the Reich-occupied territories of Poland (including Upper Silesia and the Coal Basin), could not, in his opinion, accommodate all those people who should be arrested to hinder the spread of the Polish resist-

Photo: B. Rymaszewski

Left: Group of buildings including the one in which first transport of Polish political prisoners was housed in 1940. Right: Camp watchtower, road, and track.

ance movement. He pointed to the convenient communication network of Oświęcim, as well as to the possibility of locating the

[2] Arpad Wigand, an SS-Oberführer (born in 1906), was in 1940 an inspector of the Nazi Security Service and police. In the years 1941-1942, he was an SS commander as well as the head of police in the Warsaw District. In 1947, after his extradition to Poland from the British Occupation Zone in Germany, a court in Warsaw sentenced him to 15 years in prison for war crimes.

camp away from the town, which was so densely developed that it would limit any later expansion of the camp. By using the land outside the town limits, this potential obstacle was avoided.

Despite divergent opinions, Heinrich Himmler agreed with Wigand and ordered the establishment of the Konzentrationslager Auschwitz, in Oświęcim. He also ordered that prisoners should be used as forced labor. The first commander

Photo: B. Rymaszewski

Buildings of former Polish Tobacco Company.

of the camp was Rudolf Höss, the former manager of the Sachsenhausen Camp, near Berlin.

The first group of people conscripted for the purpose of establishing the camp were 300 local Jews sent by the newly installed German mayor of the town. At the request of Höss, a group of 30 German criminals who had been prisoners of the Sachsenhausen Camp were delegated to Oświęcim and made responsible for the supervision of the other prisoners. They created the pivotal group of the notorious *kapos*, the camp supervisors renowned for their cruelty to prisoners. They constituted an important cog in the camp's mass death machine.

The camp organized in the former army barracks in Oświęcim was originally called Auschwitz. (Later, after November 1943,

Photo: B. Rymaszewski

Auschwitz admission building.

the designation changed to Auschwitz I-Stammlager: the main camp.) Upon establishment, it consisted of 20 brick buildings, most of them one-story high, in which almost 8,000 prisoners were placed in the camp's first year. Most of them were Polish.

On June 14, 1940, the first transport of 728 Polish political prisoners was brought to Auschwitz from Tarnów. They were accommodated near the railway ramp in the building of the former State Tobacco Company, which was then surrounded by a barbed wire fence, because the old army barracks were not yet prepared to house such a large number of people. As more transports were brought from other Polish cities, the prisoners were exploited for various tasks connected with the construction and development of the camp.

Photo: B. Rymaszewski

Gravel pit adjoining camp (in which SS-men shot prisoners).

The prisoners came from disparate regions of Poland and, from 1941, also from other German-occupied countries of Europe. The camp blocks were soon filled beyond capacity. The prisoners had to sleep on bunks so tightly packed that they were unable to turn to the other side. Although they were given three meals a day, the total caloric value of that food was so low that even someone doing nothing but resting would starve; needless to say, such sustenance was insufficient for people forced to toil.

The Nazis arrested people and sent them to the concentration camps for different reasons. From the occupied countries, as well as from the territories of Germany or Austria, they would send mostly those people who for political or racial reasons were considered the enemies of Nazism. The same fate befell scholars versed in the Bible, people who were "asocial and avoided work," and homosexuals. Among the imprisoned people were also some ordinary criminals, albeit these were in the minority.

Information about the existence and the nature of the Nazi camps was deliberately leaked outside the barbed wire to the occupied territories, especially to Poland and Eastern Europe. With this information, the Germans aimed to intimidate people and make them submissive. Such pieces of information contributed to the overall feeling of dread evoked by visible abuses such as public executions and street round-ups, which took place frequently in Warsaw. From time to time, certain districts of the city would be unexpectedly blocked and all the adults who were not the citizens of Germany or its allied countries were arrested and taken away.

The hostages shot in street executions and the prisoners of concentration camps were recruited from such round-ups. This, for instance, was the case of the transport of 1,666 Warsovians who reached Auschwitz on August 15, 1940. Five hundred and thirteen were first imprisoned by the Gestapo in the Pawiak prison in Warsaw, and the remaining 1,153 people were arrested in a street round-up before being sent to the camp.

Only those holders of documents certifying that they worked for institutions important to the Third Reich (e.g., in the plants whose production served the needs of the army) did not need to fear detention.

Poles, who were taken to the Nazi camps, including Auschwitz, were accused not only of their connections with the underground liberation movement. Some of them, because of their position or views, were detained because of their leadership potential and the likelihood that they might play some patriotic

Auschwitz fence, with warning board.

role. They were, for instance, clergymen or members of various Polish pre-war organizations. Numerous organizers and participants in the underground education system for children and young people were sent to German camps. Often those who dared to not comply with various ordinances of the occupational authorities were imprisoned. For example, they might be guilty of speaking Polish in public places in the Polish territories annexed by the Reich; taking part in secretly organized Chopin concerts; possessing an underground press or hidden radios, the use of which was reserved only for German Aryans.

In addition, many inhabitants of the region of Zamość were imprisoned in Auschwitz, after the Poles in that area had

Auschwitz I. Block 11, also known as "Death Block."

Photo: B. Rymaszewski

been expelled, and the land was allocated to German settlers. A similar fate was suffered by several thousand people who resided in some regions of what was then the Soviet Union, especially in the districts of Minsk and Vitebsk, which were regarded as the territories fostering partisan activities.

The Treatment of Inmates

Before the invention of gas chambers, whose average daily toll amounted to several thousand lives, the prisoners would be shot, die of starvation, or perish in extreme conditions beyond human endurance. They also died from beatings, torture, disease, and exhaustion.

Photo: B. Rymaszewski

Auschwitz I. Death wall, next to Block 11.

Inmates slept on primitive bunks, most of which were without any bedding. They were often awoken at 4:30 am and allowed to return to the barracks only late in the evening, after a day of brutally difficult labor concluded with a roll-call.

Sometimes roll-calls were deliberately prolonged and lasted as long as a dozen hours or so. More than once the prisoners

Auschwitz I. Cell in Block 11, in which Father Maksymilian Kolbe died of starvation.

were made to stand exposed to rain or frost wearing only ragged uniforms. Those who lost consciousness were mercilessly tortured. Many prisoners died in the roll-call yard either of exposure or because of the blows inflicted upon him. The same went on during the daily marches to the distant work places and on the way back to the camp. The prisoners were tortured physically and mentally.

The SS-men would shoot prisoners outside the camp fence as well as at the death wall between Blocks 10 and 11, where the camp prison was situated. The prisoners of the camp were put into it either during the investigation period or in order to serve out a penalty. On some occasions, public executions were held. These often consisted of hanging prisoners caught during attempted escapes. Such executions took place in the presence of the gathered prisoners. Sometimes death by starvation was also inflicted in special cells where prisoners were locked up with nothing to eat or drink. Among others, a person sentenced to such a death was a Franciscan monk, Maksymilian Kolbe[3], who voluntarily sacrificed his life to save a fellow-prisoner.

A large number of the camp prisoners died after being tortured with truncheons. Many others died of starvation and disease, as well as from bullets and the blows of rifle butts. The watchmen would often accuse prisoners of attempting to escape, and then beat them to death for it, because for killing a run-away, they were rewarded with some days off.

In August 1941, the SS "medical service" also started murdering prisoners. They killed the most emaciated and sick prisoners with injections of petrol, ether, or phenol. Initially, this activity was a harbinger of and later a complement to the industrialized death in the gas chambers, which started in August 1941.

The number of prisoners in Auschwitz changed constantly. This was partly due to transferring some of the prisoners to other Nazi camps, but above all, it resulted from the fact that the prisoners who died were replaced by many more new ones.

---

[3] Kolbe Rajmund (1894-1941) on joining the Franciscan monastery adopted the names Maksymilian Maria. In 1941, he was imprisoned in Auschwitz. When his fellow-prisoner, Gajowniczek, was sentenced to death, he volunteered to replace him in the starvation bunker, in which, after several days of torment, he was killed with a phenol injection. In the Catholic Church, he was beatified in 1971, and in 1982 he was canonized as a martyr saint – Father Maksymilian Kolbe.

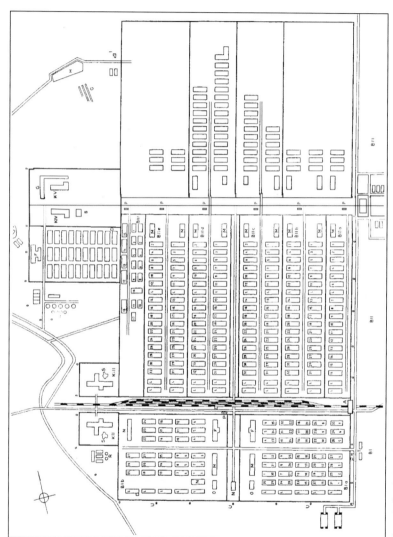

Photo: A. Strzelecka-Jasiewicz

Plan of Auschwitz II-Birkenau, by A Strzelecka-Jasiewicz.

Auschwitz II-Birkenau.

A	Main SS-guardhouse.
BI	First section of camp.
BIa	Camp for female prisoners of various nationalities.
BIb	Camp for prisoners of various nationalities; later for women prisoners.
BII	Second section of camp.
BIIa	Quarantine camp for prisoners of various nationalities.
BIIb	Family camp for Jews from Terezin ghetto.
BIIc	Transitory camp for Jewish women, mostly from Hungary.
BIId	Camp for male prisoners of various nationalities.
BIIe	Family camp for Gypsies.
BIIf	Hospital for male prisoners.
BIII	Third section of camp (not completed); so-called "Mexico": transitory camp for Jewish women, mostly from Hungary.
C	Headquarters and SS barracks.
D	Warehouses with confiscated possessions of inmates; so-called "Canada" II.
E	Sidetrack and railway ramp, where deported people were brought after May 1944; place where Jews were selected, or sorted.
F	Bathhouses and site of admission for new transports.
G	Open-air area where bodies were incinerated.
H	Mass graves of Soviet prisoners of war.
I	First, makeshift gas chamber.
KII, KIII, KIV, KV	Crematoria II, III, IV, V, and gas chambers.
L	Latrines and lavatories.
M	Kitchens.
N	Warehouses.
O	Buildings where potatoes were peeled.
P	SS guardhouse.
R	Purifiers.
S	Places where ashes of the dead were heaped.
T	Exit quarantine for female prisoners.
U	Watchtowers.

Prisoners' barracks are marked with Arabic numerals. In the bottom part of the BIa section, some of the barracks retain numbering introduced in 1944; in corresponding BIb section, original numbering is used.

Auschwitz II-Birkenau, aerial view.

Photo: W. Gorgolewski, 1996

Auschwitz II-Birkenau: The Primary Site for the Extermination of European Jewry

Development of physical plant

After March 1941, in accordance with Himmler's orders, Auschwitz expanded significantly. Plans were to develop it to accommodate 30,000 prisoners. However, preparations for the invasion of the Soviet Union made the authorities in Berlin decide to build a new camp, Auschwitz II-Birkenau, in the village of Brzezinka, situated 3 kilometers from Oświęcim. The latter camp was earmarked for about 100,000 prisoners of war.

The Polish population of Brzezinka and of other nearby villages was summarily evicted by the SS-men. The abandoned households were then pulled down by prisoners who were also forced to build the camp, using, among other materials, the remnants of the demolished villages. They had to build the barbed wire fence, watchtowers, prisoners' barracks, storehouses, kitchens, latrines, sewage and land reclamation systems, roads, and other facilities, including the army barracks and recreational facilities for the SS staff. Slave labor was also exploited during the construction of the gas chambers and crematoria, as well as of the railway ramp.

In this way, an area of about 170 hectares was developed into the huge complex known as Auschwitz II-Birkenau, in which, at one time in 1944, 90,000 people were imprisoned and distributed in separate sections of the camp: the male sections, the female sections, the family sections, and the temporary sections.

Shift in function

Besides the long-term extermination and exploitation function of a typical Nazi work camp, in 1942, Auschwitz started playing the role of an immense German death camp. As a part of the Nazi plan for the final solution of the Jewish problem, it became the principal place for murdering the Jews from the territories

Auschwitz II-Birkenau. Block 27. Currently housing a permanent exhibition of Jewish martyrology.

of the Reich and of these European countries that were either under German occupation or in alliance with the Reich. The Nazis intended to kill everyone, irrespective of their age and sex, who had any Jewish roots going as far back as three generations.

Before World War II, more than 3 million Jews lived in Poland; this constituted the largest Jewish population in Europe. During the German occupation, the majority were murdered by the Nazis, mostly in the death camps at Treblinka, Bełżec, Sobibor, Chełmno upon Ner, and Auschwitz, in the ghettos, as well as in numerous places of mass and individual executions.

Among the Jews deported to Auschwitz and killed in the gas chambers of Birkenau, the most numerous group, amounting to about 438,000, were Hungarian Jews. There were also about 300,000 Polish Jews. The remaining Jews were brought from France (around 69,000), Holland (60,000), Greece (55,000), Bohemia (46,000), Slovakia (27,000), Belgium (25,000), Austria and Germany (23,000), Yugoslavia (10,000), Italy (7,500), Norway (around 690 people); there were also 34,000 people from other camps.

The first groups of Jews were probably brought to the camps in cars as early as 1941, and they were executed almost immediately. The mass procedure of bringing to and murdering in Auschwitz whole Jewish families from German-occupied or German-dependent countries lasted 3 years. Nearly 80% of these people died in gas chambers directly after their arrival at the ramp. After the selection at the ramp, the remaining 20 percent of these people who were found suitable for being used in the labor force were registered in the camp files. This meant only the postponement of death because in Auschwitz, people also lost their lives as a result of the extremely harsh living conditions.

Apart from the Jews, the victims of the gas chambers included Gypsies, Soviet captives, and some Polish prisoners.

Development of gas chambers and crematoria

The first crematorium was started in Auschwitz in August 1940, in the former ammunition bunker that used to belong to the army barracks. In the autumn of the following year, a gas chamber was built next to it. The first people to be killed in it were 900 Soviet captives and then a group of Jews from Upper Silesia. Gassing in Auschwitz I continued till the end of 1942, and the incineration of the bodies lasted till July 1943. Later, the building was converted into an air-raid shelter for the SS staff.

From spring 1942, the gassing of the prisoners was done in Auschwitz II-Birkenau, in two little country houses referred to as bunkers. They were situated close to the camp, and they

Photo: B. Rymaszewski

Auschwitz I. Gas chamber and crematorium in former ammunition bunker.

served as makeshift gas chambers. No crematoria were built there. The dead bodies were buried in the fields allocated for that purpose. Later, in order to obliterate the traces of the crime, the bodies were dug up and burned.

The transports of Jews, sent to death in Auschwitz from 1942, were directed to the railway siding. There, the people would be brutally driven to a ramp, while a selection process was carried out, against the accompanying noise of the SS-men's screams and of the barking of dogs. During any selection procedure, the SS physicians separated physically fit people into a group designated to augment the constantly decreasing labor force.

Everyone was divested of luggage, told to undress, and go naked to the bath. But only those who were chosen as fit for various kinds of slave labor were taken to a real bathhouse. There, after registration, they were given prisoners' uniforms and delegated to various groups.

The remaining people were squeezed into rooms that looked like bathhouses. In fact, these were gas chambers in which, within several minutes, the people died from inhaling cyclone B gas. Granules of cyclone B were thrown in through special openings by SS-men who were wearing gas masks to protect themselves from poisoning.

In the first half of 1943, the construction of four large gas chambers with crematoria was completed in Auschwitz II-Birkenau. These sections of the death factory were marked II, III, IV, and V. The process of killing was accelerated. In the peak periods of mass murders, the daily toll was about 12,000 lives. Such numbers exceeded the technical capacity of the crematoria, so parallel to the industrial incineration; the bodies were also burned outside.

The activities connected with carrying and cremating bodies were performed, under supervision, by a special group of prisoners, called *Sonderkommando*. Other groups were responsible for storing and sorting confiscated valuables and other things, including the gold obtained from the extracted teeth of the dead, all of which was later sent to the Reich. The ashes from the cremated bodies were taken on trolleys to specified places situated near the crematoria. Ashes were also thrown into the camp pond, as well as into the nearby Vistula and Soła Rivers. Some of the ashes were also used for fertilizing the cultivated land of the SS.

The prisoners of the *Sonderkommando* were also eventually killed in gas chambers because they were inconvenient witnesses to the crimes of the camp. Their places were taken by the new ones, usually chosen from the newly arrived transports.

Auschwitz II-Birkenau. Pond in which the ashes of the dead were dumped.

In October 1944, in the face of death, a group of Jewish prisoners chosen to run Crematorium IV rebelled in desperation and killed three of the supervising SS-men. Then they set about destroying the gas chamber and the crematorium. The attempted escape was, however, unsuccessful. As a result of the immediate counter-action of the camp staff, 450 prisoners from the *Sonderkommando* were caught and executed.

Later the camp Gestapo arrested four Jewish women-prisoners who had supplied explosives to the participants of the desperate mutiny. These women had succeeded in purloining the explosives and smuggling them from a factory outside the camp in which they were employed. After an investigation, the women

Auschwitz II-Birkenau. Fence facing town of Oświęcim.

were hanged in the presence of their fellow prisoners in what was the last public execution before the liberation of the camp.

Attempts to tally the victims

It is impossible to establish the exact number of the Nazi Holocaust victims in Auschwitz because the executioners did not keep any registers of those people who were murdered directly after their arrival at the camp. After selections, the majority of the Jews were directed to gas chambers without anyone bothering to write down their personal data. That is why the numbers of the camp victims are only estimated on the basis of the transportation lists of deported people.

Auschwitz I. Main gate.

Photo: L. Foryciarz

In spite of recent progress in research methods and means, it is unlikely that it will ever become possible to identify and count the victims, whose only remaining traces are their ashes. The memory of those who survived is dimmed by the passing of time, while the archive sources confronted with the evidence of the witnesses allow us to establish only an approximate number of victims, which is still an outrageous number.

On Both Sides of the Gate Inscribed Arbeit macht frei

How prisoners were abused and utilized

As noted earlier, only those prisoners who survived selection were registered in the camp files. They were assigned numbers, which were used instead of their names and surnames. Tattooed on the prisoners' forearms, these numbers were also placed on their uniforms, next to a triangle, which was a mark distinguishing a prisoner's category (e.g., political, including the nationality, or asocial, criminal, and others). Jews were marked with the yellow Star of David.

Only very few prisoners were sentenced in accordance with Nazi law. The majority got there without any such procedure. In most cases, however, the stay ended in death.

The guiding principle was that people should be killed quickly for reasons of economy. This concerned particularly Jews, Gypsies, and some Slavs, especially those, irrespective of their age and sex, who were considered dangerous to the Third Reich. With that idea in mind, the Nazis developed not only a cost-effective way of gassing people but also an equally effective means of making use of all the things left behind by the dead that could be used by the German economy.

These items included everything taken away from victims before they were killed: valuables, money, suitcases, clothes, shoes, glasses, toothbrushes, combs, shaving brushes, prostheses, baby prams, pots, and other objects of everyday use. The Nazis tried hard to make use even of the hair and ashes of the people murdered in the camps, the Jews in particular.

According to Nazi plans, the prisoners without particular skill sets were to be exploited as the cheapest possible labor force. During World War II, and in particular in its final

SUB-CAMPS OF AUSCHWITZ CONCENTRATION CAMP

Contents © by Franciszek Piper
Graphic design © by Pawel Warchol

years, the economy of Nazi Germany was partly based on slave labor. In addition to people deported against their will to forced labor in Germany, the prisoners of the concentration camps were forced into slave labor. They were mostly employed in the armaments, chemical, electrical, and metal industries, as well as in mining and other hard work, such as in agriculture.

This labor force was to fill the staffing vacancies in the economy, which resulted from allied bombings and from the fact that almost all Germans capable of military service had been directly mobilized and involved in the war machine. Almost as many as 40 prisoners' sub camps were created in the area of Oświęcim, near major industrial plants, steelworks, mines, and farms. Thus Auschwitz III-Monowitz

Photo: B. Rymaszewski

Auschwitz I (Stammlager). Demarcation line between prisoners' section and SS section.

was established in Monowice, where an entirely new, immense chemical plant was being built. Among others, it was to produce synthetic petrol and rubber. Until October 1943, other sub camps were subject to that camp.

The managing SS staff at Auschwitz collected fees from the factories for the slave labor of the prisoners. Part of that income, like the gold and valuables stolen from the prisoners, subsidized the treasury of the Third Reich.

The industrial plants and farms belonging to the SS were also based on the forced labor of prisoners. They covered an immense area of almost 4,000 hectares, which was referred to as *Interessengebiet*, or, in other words, the "camp area of interests," which constituted the economic territory of the SS. After the majority of the former inhabitants of that zone had been evicted, access to it from the outside was strictly controlled.

Mostly women prisoners worked in the arable fields adjoining the camp. They were also involved in land improvement tasks, road repairs, and in breeding animals. Like the men and children imprisoned in the camp, women were also minimally nourished, beaten, and chased by dogs. While their supervisors were screaming at them, they had to do work beyond their abilities. They were force-marched to their places of work, which were sometimes situated many kilometers away. The working conditions were primitive. The prisoners did not have proper clothes, and sometimes they had to work barefooted and with simple tools. Many died while they worked.

To demonstrate a so-called respect for the law, the Nazis released some prisoners from the camp after they had served their sentences. This concerned as few as 1,500 people, only a small fraction of the total number of prisoners. Although the inscription above the gate to Auschwitz I announced that "Work makes you free," the prisoners exposed to that slogan knew well enough that it had nothing to do with a promise of freedom in return for toil. Even eagerness in performing the slave work in the camp offered not the slightest hope of being released. Death threatened the prisoners all over the camp, and only death could offer eventual liberation.

People en route to Auschwitz in fact stood little chance of surviving. However, many of them could at least cherish the hope that it was not the final journey of their lives. Most West European Jews were not really aware of the

Auschwitz II-Birkenau at dusk.

Photo: B. Rymaszewski

actual danger, especially because the Nazis loading them into the transports spoke only of displacement. Some Poles, Russians, and Ukrainians, on the other hand, could also delude themselves. They were not immediately shot or hanged even though the punishment established by the Third Reich was immediate execution for most so-called offences committed by the inhabitants of occupied Poland and of the lands situated to the east of it. Such penalties were common in the occupied territories, among others, for helping or hiding Jews, for possessing weapons, or for stealing German property.

How the camp was supervised

In the first phase of the organization of Auschwitz, in May 1940, a dozen or so SS-men were delegated to Oświęcim. As the first team of watchmen, they were the camp's original staff, which, after a month, already consisted of 100 privates, noncommissioned officers, and officers, all of them with death-head insignia on their caps. As the camp expanded, the staff increased to about 3,000. The garrison was armed with numerous machine guns to assist the staff's supervision of the prisoners in the camp and outside it.

The SS unit in Auschwitz constituted a considerable military force sufficient for suppressing a possible rebellion of the thousands of prisoners or to fend off an external attack. In addition, it was guaranteed back up by the Wermacht troops billeted near by. For these reasons, the leadership of the Polish underground decided against an attempt to liberate the prisoners through a direct attack by partisan troops. The resistance estimated that even if there were a chance of defeating the well-armed SS-men, it would be impossible to lead out and hide safely 100,000 exhausted prisoners. Thus, resistance activities focused primarily on smuggling food, medicine, and information to the prisoners and helping them with escape attempts.

In spite of the well-developed supervision system, at least 144 successful escapes from the camp and from the working places outside it took place between June 1940 and January 1945. There were also several hundred attempted escapes. Polish underground organizations, as well as a large part of the local Polish population, helped the escapees, though the punishment for this was death. The SS-men responded to all the successful and unsuccessful escapes with repression in order to intimidate other prisoners, to make them submissive

Photo: B. Rymaszewski

Auschwitz II-Birkenau. Wooden barracks.

and, in general, to make the task of supervising the prisoners easier.

Other means were employed to discourage prisoners from attempts to escape. All the prisoners had to do exhausting work. There were, however, some jobs that were considered better and some that were worse. Some were performed indoors and some out of doors. Some made it possible to move freely in the camp and have access to food or drugs. Some of the prisoners had a chance of survival because of being employed indoors, for instance, in the kitchen or in the warehouses. Being assigned to the camp fire brigade, which was also used for extinguishing fires outside the camp, created possibilities to get better clothes and larger food

Auschwitz II-Birkenau. Inside a wooden barrack.

rations. Additional portions of food were also given to some selected prisoners who were entrusted with supervising functions.

Creating privileged posts for prisoners, as well as differentiating the conditions of life in various groups, helped the SS-men to govern the enslaved community. The SS-men aimed to antagonize the large community imprisoned by the wires, which consisted of individuals and whole groups differing not only in their nationalities, but also in religion, age, political views, education levels, and social and moral status. The Nazi attempts to create inner discrepancies among the prisoners remained unsuccessful. Instead, individuals and groups who were opponents when free, now became closer

Auschwitz II-Birkenau. Inner railway ramp, where selections were conducted.

to each other. Among such instances, is the case of a pre-war anti-Semitic leader of the Polish nationalist movement who helped his Jewish fellow-prisoners in the camp. After he had been put in Auschwitz, he became actively involved in the prisoners' resistance movement, whose task, among others, was to enhance the solidarity of the prisoners.

The bonds of intra-camp resistance were repeatedly strained, however, by the death and by transfer of prisoners to other camps. Such transfers involved about 200,000 prisoners and within this number were many secret members of the camp underground. Members of the underground offered help to fellow-prisoners with political, cultural, religious, and even military support. The latter involved preparations

Photo: B. Rymaszewski

Auschwitz II-Birkenau. View of main guardhouse and inner railway ramp as seen from the International Monument of the Victims of the Extermination Camp.

for active fighting in case some favorable conditions should emerge.

The main emphasis was on counteracting the mental and moral collapse of prisoners, and on collecting and passing to the outside world information about the torture and crimes committed in the camp. In addition, prisoners were given food, drugs, and clothes obtained with much effort. Thanks to the maintenance of sophisticated connections with the Polish underground organizations, it was possible to circulate in the camp some pieces of information concerning the fighting with Germany. This uplifted the spirits of the prisoners.

Many prisoners were involved in the camp conspiracy. Following the patterns of the underground organizations acti-

Auschwitz II-Birkenau. First section of camp.

ve in the occupied territories, it was based on the system of trios or fives that consisted of Polish, Jewish, Austrian and German, Yugoslavian, French, Czech, Russian, and other groups.

There were some partly successful attempts to consolidate and create a uniform leadership of the camp resistance movement. One such organizer was an officer of the Polish underground, Witold Pilecki[4], who under a false name, with the consent of his superiors, deliberately let himself be caught in a street round-up in Warsaw in September 1940. He entered Auschwitz in order to gather information about the mass murders committed there. In 1943, he escaped from the camp and provided reliable information about the actual role of the camp and the torturers employed there. His testimony, together with the information passed subsequently through conspirational channels, were later included in the reports of the headquarters of the Polish underground in Warsaw (Home Army Headquarters[5] and the Delegates of the Government of the Polish Republic in the Country[6]). They were used in the dispatches sent to London by secret radio stations.

[4] Witold Pilecki (1901-1948) a reserve officer of the Polish Army, a participant of the war of 1920 and 1939. During the occupation period he was a cofounder of the Polish Secret Army (of which he was later leader), which later joined the Association of Armed Struggle and later the Home Army. During his stay in Auschwitz, he was one of the promoters of the secret Association of Military Organizations that coordinated the conspiratorial activities of some prisoners. After his escape from the camp, he rejoined the resistance movement and cooperated with the Home Army Headquarters. He fought in the Warsaw Uprising and after the capitulation, he found himself in a camp for prisoners of war. He came back to Poland in December 1945. In 1947, he was arrested and tried for espionage activities and working for the Polish emigration authorities in London. He was sentenced to death and executed.

[5] Home Army, the largest Polish underground organization, which in the final years of the German occupation had as many as 300,000 or more active members. It carried out the armed struggle against the occupying forces through partisan and conspiratorial units and, from summer 1944, also in the form of insurgents' units as a part of the Storm action. It was established on February 14, 1942, pursuant to the order of General Władysław Sikorski, the Commander-in-Chief and the Prime Minister of the Government in Exile (in London). He worked for the consolidation of the entire Polish armed resistance movement, which at that time consisted of about 300 organizations. The strongest of them was the Association of Armed Struggle, created in January 1940 out of the Polish Victory Service, created as early as September 1939.

[6] Delegates of the Government of the Polish Republic in the Country constituted in occupied Warsaw a conspiratorial representation of the Polish Government in London (in exile). It was an underground representation of the major political parties. The Leadership of Civilian Struggle was active within it from 1941. It initiated sabotage

More extensive reports were smuggled by secret couriers, especially by Jan Karski[7], who informed the governments of Great Britain and of the United States about the Holocaust of the Jews conducted by the Germans in the occupied territories of Poland. As noted earlier, the number of Auschwitz prisoners changed continuously. For instance, in 1944, in January, there were

Photo: B. Rymaszewski

Auschwitz II-Birkenau. Ruins of makeshift gas chamber (Bunker 2).

---

actions, recorded the Holocaust and other crimes committed by the occupying forces, coordinated the passive resistance of Polish society and tried traitors. Reports including the data concerning war criminals were drawn up. Their most essential parts were sent to London either through secret radio stations or through secret couriers.

[7] Dr. Jan Kozielewski (1914-2000) a reserve lieutenant in the Polish Army, and from 1939, an employee of the Ministry of Foreign Affairs. During the occupation, he used the codename Jan Karski and he was the famous secret courier of the Headquarters of the Association of Armed Struggle and the Home Army. Via Paris he smuggled confidential documents from occupied Warsaw to London. In 1943, he personally reported to the President of the United States, Franklin Roosevelt, about the Holocaust of European Jews.

80,839; in July 92,208; and in August more than 135,000. In the last, general roll-call, held on January 17, 1945, 67,012 prisoners Auschwitz I, II-Birkenau and III-Monowitz participated. Already in the second half of 1944, taking into account the possible offensive on the eastern front, the Nazis undertook some actions aimed at obliterating the evidence of their crimes. They would burn documents and empty the large warehouses of the things taken away from the inmates.

Auschwitz I. Museum exhibit of glasses of murdered inmates.

In fear of the forthcoming breaking of the front and the rapid approach of the Soviet Army toward Oświęcim, in November 1944, they stopped sending transports of Jews to Auschwitz. Before their eventual escape, the SS-men managed to blow up the gas chambers and crematoria. In freezing weather, they then drove westward thousands of prisoners. After the prisoners had walked a considerable distance from the camp, they were loaded into railway goods-carriages in which they were to reach their destinations in other camps. Before arriving elsewhere, however, many prisoners died of exhaustion or were killed by the escorting SS-men. After the war, the many-kilometer long Death March Route in Poland was commemorated with memorial plaques and simple monuments. This was the way of com-

Photo: B. Rymaszewski

Auschwitz I. View of crematorium, gas chamber, and guardhouse.

memorating thousands of Auschwitz prisoners who breathed their last far away from the camp, but who were still its victims.

On January 27, 1945, the 7,000 or so prisoners left behind in the camp were liberated by the Soviet soldiers of the 100th infantry division of the 60th army of the 1st Ukrainian Front, which dislodged the Germans from Oświęcim.

THE AUSCHWITZ CONCENTRATION CAMP ECONOMIC "INTEREST ZONE" (INTERESSENGEBIET)

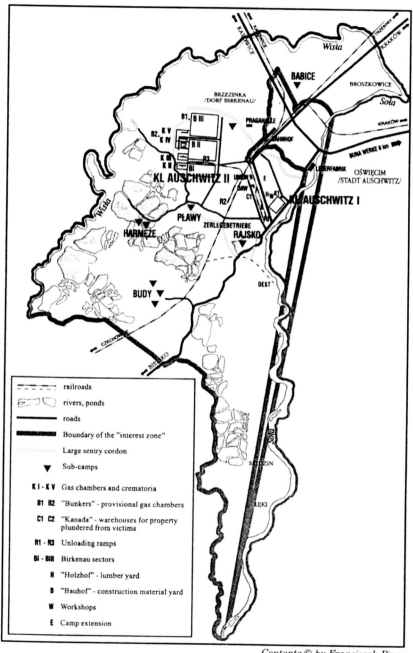

Legend:

- ---- railroads
- rivers, ponds
- —— roads
- ▬▬▬ Boundary of the "interest zone"
- .... Large sentry cordon
- ▼ Sub-camps
- **K I - K V** Gas chambers and crematoria
- **B1 B2** "Bunkers" - provisional gas chambers
- **C1 C2** "Kanada" - warehouses for property plundered from victims
- **R1 - R3** Unloading ramps
- **BI - BIII** Birkenau sectors
- **H** "Holzhof" - lumber yard
- **B** "Bauhof" - construction material yard
- **W** Workshops
- **E** Camp extension

Contents © by Franciszek Piper
Graphic design © by Paweł Warchoł

After the Liberation of the Camp

In order to strengthen the resolve of the soldiers toward the end of World War II, the various headquarters of the allied forces, especially in the East, spread information about the crimes committed by the Nazis in the concentration camps. Stalinist propaganda, for example, focused on the widest spectrum of the Nazi crimes in order to divert attention from the crimes for which Stalin and his own system of violence were responsible. Widely publicized were the numerous, "fresh" traces of crimes discovered by the units of the Red Army dislodging the Germans from the occupied territories.

Within the borders of present-day Poland, which lost more than 6,000,000 citizens, about half of whom were of Jewish descent, the German forces had organized almost 6,000 camps and prisons. As it happened, the largest number of crimes was committed at Auschwitz. The surviving camp buildings and equipment, the ashes of the murdered, as well as their personal belongings constituted an unambiguous testimony to crimes committed there. That is why the allied special services, which followed the frontline troops of the Soviet Army, cooperated with the Commission for Investigating German Crimes in trying to secure the evidence, including the large quantities of human hair, shoes, and other objects belonging to the victims, as well as camp documents that the SS-men did not have time to destroy.

Soon after the frontline had moved west of Oświęcim, the newly organized Polish administration made sure that the surviving buildings of Auschwitz were not spontaneously destroyed. This supervision was simplified by the fact that some of the camp buildings were used temporarily for interning German prisoners of war. However, there was no clear and generally accepted idea of what to do with such a large complex as Auschwitz.

Auschwitz I. Watchtower and farm building.

The same hesitation surrounded the disposition of other places of mass death from the years of World War II. Because of the tragedies, some people favored complete destruction of all evidence of that nightmare. They insisted on dismantling all the camp buildings and constructions and planting a forest over the entire area, including the ashes of the murdered.

This forest was to be a kind of symbol of the rebirth of life. However, people realized early enough that such a solution would not pay due homage to the victims but rather would bring about gradual oblivion instead.

In February 1945, in the territories of Poland liberated from the German occupation, the Organizational Committee for the Construction of the Museum Monument in Oświęcim

Auschwitz II-Birkenau. Fragments of the ruins of Crematorium II.

Photo: B. Rymaszwski

was established. Addressing the new Polish central authorities, which had become active in Lublin in July 1944, the committee demanded that, "in honor of the memory of the Forefathers and as a warning for the Brothers," and in order to commemorate the victims of the Death Camp, "a Monument-Museum and a burial mound should be created ...."

It was suggested that the immense shelter bunker in the town of Oświęcim would be excellent. The need to commemorate the events was explained by the fact that "the passing of time would dry out the orphans' tears, soothe the pain and heal the inflicted wounds. The boundless suffering of the Forefathers would for posterity become only an Old Tale."

Auschwitz II-Birkenau. Ruins of gas chamber and Crematorium II.

The committee here referred to the title of a popular novel by Józef Ignacy Kraszewski[8], published for the first time in

---

[8] Józef Ignacy Kraszewski (1812-1887) – Poland's most popular romantic historical writer. He was the author of 232 novels most of which were devoted to the history of Poland. Among them was *The Old Tale* published many times in large numbers. It popularized the early history of the Polish state known mostly from legends.

1876, in which the author freely improvised on the events from the early history of Poland. At one time, the book had been obligatory reading for school. Although it had the power of stirring imagination, and it stimulated interest in the history of Poland, it was by no means a reliable historical source.

Similarly, the social initiative concerning the construction of the monument stemmed from emotions and was aimed only

Photo: B. Rymaszewski

Auschwitz II-Birkenau. Ruins of gas chamber and Crematorium II. Prisoners' barracks in the background.

at symbolic commemoration of the camp victims and not at preserving the authentic evidence of the crime.

During this debate, fighting was still occurring in the western parts of Poland, which were still in the hands of the Third Reich, and in which numerous camps were still operational.

The people attempting to establish a monument at Auschwitz were sensitive and free of the desire for revenge. They mounted exhibitions in the last months of the war showing the Nazi crimes committed in Auschwitz, in Majdanek, and in other execution places.

Early in 1945, the Division of Museums and Monuments of Polish Martyrology was created in the Main Department of Museums and Protection of Monuments at the Ministry of Culture and Art. Its activities focused on various forms of protection of the material evidence of martyrdom that took place in the territories of Poland. In the political situation at that time, those could concern only commemorating the Nazi crimes, although the Poles had also suffered immense losses as a result of the Stalinist regime.

The tasks of the newly appointed division were neither easy nor typical. Poland was ruined by the war and occupation, and Polish society, in trying hard to rebuild its world, was involved, both actively and emotionally, in serious political struggle. Bloodshed would often occur and prisons, as well as some of the camps abandoned by the Germans, were filled with the opponents of the Russian system. For several years after 1945, in one of the former subcamps of Auschwitz, at Jaworzno, imprisoned amongst others, were some members of the Polish resistance movement from the Home Army[9], which was earlier involved in fighting against the German forces.

---

[9] The last commander-in-chief of the Home Army was Brigade General Leopold Okulicki (using the codename – "Niedźwiadek", meaning Teddy), who formally dissolved that large underground organization and its partisan troops by an order issued on January 19, 1945. Many of its members, after having come out into the open, were arrested. Quite a number of them were executed, while many others were deported to the Soviet Union. That was one of the basic reasons for re-establishing the former and creating the new units of the armed underground movement and for carrying out the struggle against the system of power, imposed and actively supported by the Soviet security forces and the Soviet Army. General Okulicki, together with 15 other members of the Polish authorities from the time of the German occupation, was perfidiously arrested by Soviet secret agents on March 23, 1945. He was then taken to Moscow where he was tried and imprisoned and where he died in unknown circumstances.

After World War II, in Poland, as in some other countries, there emerged a need to commemorate the places of suffering and death. Auschwitz was an obvious example. The awareness of the need to protect this monument of martyrology from destruction was shared by many of its former prisoners and their families. That conviction existed also among many Polish conservators of historic monuments and museum experts.

Auschwitz I. Brick blocks.

The employees of the Ministry of Culture and Art, especially in the first years after the war, were, however, unable to create on their own an effective protection system encompassing all that was left of Auschwitz. For instance, it was impossible to stop the dismantling of the wooden barracks in Birkenau. Those former army stables, passed over to the camp by the

Wermacht forces, functioned in the camp as dwellings for prisoners and as storehouses. After being taken down, they were transported to Warsaw, where they were reassembled and used by the Youth Working Teams. It happened in this way because in Warsaw, reduced by the Nazis to a heap of rubble, even the most primitive shelter was very useful.

On the initiative of the Ministry of Culture and Art, which among others was concerned with putting an end to the dismantling actions in the camp area, the Polish Seym (Parliament) passed several laws on July 2, 1947. One of them provided for the establishment of the Council for the Protection of Martyrdom Monuments, which in 1949 was transformed into the Council for the Protection of Struggle and Martyrdom Monuments, and in 1987 into the Council for the Protection of the Memory of Struggle and Martyrdom. The drafts of three other laws worked out in 1947 were concerned with commemorating the martyrdom of the Polish nation and of other nations in the former camps in Oświęcim, Majdanek, and Treblinka. The first two laws were passed, while the third draft was withdrawn, probably following an order from the highest political leadership.

Therefore, legal acts of the highest status were decisive for creating state museums in Oświęcim and Majdanek, and they enabled the Ministry of Culture and Art to specify their areas as well as the organizational framework. In other words, the Seym created a legal obstacle for the trend manifesting itself in the devastation of the area of the former camps and adaptation of the buildings for various purposes. That tendency was connected with the general ruin of the country and scarcity of buildings suitable for any use. That situation was partly accounted for in the first draft of the Oświęcim law, which provided for locating in the area of the former camp not only the State Museum but also the Center of Vocational Training of the Polish Youth.

Promises were made that the center would grant priority to the children and orphans of the former political prisoners

Photo: B. Rymaszewski

Auschwitz I. Demarcation zone between camp proper and SS section.

of Nazi prisons and concentration camps. Eventually, however, the museum-oriented version of the law was passed and no vocational training was conducted behind the derisive inscription *Arbeit macht frei.*

Photo: B. Rymaszewski

Auschwitz II-Birkenau. Watchtower.

Cemetery

Auschwitz is believed to be one of the largest cemeteries in the world. It is an unusual cemetery, however, in that the dead were deprived not only of the right to a tomb but also to an undisturbed place of eternal rest.

In the first years of the camp's operation, the mixed remains of the registered and killed prisoners after cremation, were, according to the Nazi procedure, placed in urns and sent to home addresses together with a certificate of death, almost always stating a fake cause of death. By the decision of the Inspectorate of the Concentration Camps of April 17, 1941, the distribution of the ashes of Poles was stopped. The same edict referred to the distribution of the ashes of Russian, Jewish, and Gypsy prisoners. Thus, huge quantities of ashes remained near the site of the crime. At present, it is difficult to define what quantity of ashes was dumped into a pond near the crematoria within Auschwitz II-Birkenau or which were piled nearby. It is known that the majority of ashes were taken by the rivers or spread by the wind onto the farming fields and gardens belonging to SS officers.

It is no longer possible to indicate the places of eternal rest of particular people, either in the known areas of storage within the camp or in the immediate vicinity. This is also the case in terms of where Russian prisoners of war were buried, outside the fence, near the north-western corner of Auschwitz II-Birkenau. Although 8,000 names of the murdered soldiers of the Red Army have been verified, there is no possibility of individual identification of particular remains. They lie in a large common tomb as thousands of unknown soldiers and victims of the death camp.

In the area of Auschwitz II-Birkenau, it is also impossible to clearly mark the places where the ashes of particular Gypsies were buried, although almost all their names are known. Entire families were murdered, as happened to the Jews; for the Gypsies, the reasons were racial rather than religious.

Within the death camp, human ashes have been completely mixed together with the soil. No one will ever be able to separate the remains of the Poles, Jews, Gypsies, Russians, Yugoslavs, or several other nationalities representing various cultures and traditions, ideas, religions, and professions. A common tragic fate bound them together, inseparably, blurring any differences between them.

The area of Auschwitz II-Birkenau and the regions where ashes are buried are now covered with greenery. This natural exuberance is tempered each year by custodians who dig up the bushes and cut the grass. The camp area seen in beautiful weather looks peaceful and does not remind one of the previous grimness.

Relatives of the victims try to visit the places of eternal rest of their families, and, according to their customs, leave material traces of remembrance. Who is, however, able to tell for certain where the ashes of individual people were buried? The only solution is to commemorate entire communities while respecting individual intentions.

In some ways, as resting place, the camp cemetery is similar to the oceans. Two major differences lie in the scale of the anonymous mass of ashes.

During discussions in the Polish cultural press of the future of the postcamp area in 1950, the particular nature of the cemetery was a source of contention. In *Tygodnik Powszechny*, a Polish weekly, Jan Paweł Gawlik[10], supported by

Photo: B. Rymaszewski

Auschwitz II-Birkenau. Ashes of victims.

Eugenia Kocwa[11], suggested that crosses should be erected in Auschwitz, with the number matching that of the number of

---

[10] Jan Paweł Gawlik (b. in 1924, Kraków publicist, theatre specialist and critic), in an article "Odpowiedź na wątpliwości" , *Tygodnik Powszechny*, no 58, 1950.

[11] Eugenia Kocwa (1907-1963, writer, publicist, and academic at the Jagiellonian University in Kraków), in article "Oświęcimskie krzyże", *Tygodnik Powszechny*, no 27, 1950.

people murdered there. The idea did not take into account cultural variation in creating cemeteries: Whereas erecting crosses was respectful of Christian culture, most victims of Auschwitz were Jewish, and Judaism honors its dead in a different way.

The proposal also did not take into account the role of the former camp as a vital piece of physical evidence. Most of all, it was impossible to implement. The number of people murdered in Auschwitz was so great that there is not enough open area to honor every person even with the most modest grave.

Eugenia Kocwa was ambivalent regarding the decision to create a museum in the camp. She viewed Auschwitz primarily as a cemetery. She wrote that many people were shocked at the thought of creating a museum, as they believed it would profane the site.

Zofia Bączkowska[12], in the same weekly, proposed an idea that was far from realistic, yet it took into account the conceptual significance of the place. The author suggested that the postcamp area should become something between a monument and a cemetery of nations, and she suggested the creation of what she called *Campo Santo – A Sacred Field*, where each nation could erect an appropriate monument. She did not precisely define the location of this sacred field and did not suggest the use of what was left of the camp. She only expressed the opinion that Oświęcim might become a place of pilgrimage and serve to propagate peace. The article reminded readers of the need to respect many

---

[12] Zofia Bączkowska "Oświęcim wiecznie żywy", *Tygodnik Powszechny*, no. 29, 1950.

Photo: B. Rymaszewski

Auschwitz I. The camp admission building.

cultures and to value mutual kindness, especially among those societies whose representatives had become victims of intolerance.

The opinions presented here represent part of the search toward a definition of the present role of Auschwitz. Similar to other death camps, Auschwitz has a dual meaning: It is a great cemetery, an area partly covered with the ashes of the dead. It is also an area where a terrible crime was committed and, therefore, it documents this crime. The need to take into account both these aspects suggests that no trappings typical of cemeteries should be present within the camp area. They are excluded by the differences of the religious requirements, mainly Jewish and Christian, but also Muslim, as some of the people murdered here represented this religion. Moreover, the construction of a cemetery, in the full meaning of the word, would collide with the preservation of the historical landscape.

Honoring the varied expectations of the families and relatives of the victims is warranted, of course, but it does not mean that within the area enclosed by the wire fence, the custodians should search for a place to locate plates, graves, or chapels. Such proposals are bound to face the dilemmas of the need to find appropriate proportions for displaying the signs of representative religions as well as to decide on the possible places for their distribution. Moreover, the Jews exclude the possibility of sharing their cemetery area with cemeteries of other religions and do not construct houses of prayer there. They also oppose the transfers of the remains of the Jews from the places of their initial burial.

Most important, there is no possibility of creating any formal cemeteries in the camp area without infringing on its documentary value. However, preserving the area with human ashes in the authentic landscape, free from reconstructions and visible new arrangements, allows visitors to experience an authentic encounter. The preservation of the area with the historical content related to the martyrs of the largest death plant of the 20th century naturally encourages contemplation and prayer.

Photo: B. Rymaszewski

Auschwitz II-Birkenau. The remains of the gas chamber and crematorium IV.

Auschwitz II-Birkenau. The central part of the International Monument of the Victims of the Death Camp.

Historical Monument and Monument

The two terms – *historical monument* and *monument* (*zabytek, pomnik*) – may look unnecessarily repetitive to an English or German reader. And, in general, in languages other than Polish, only one word is used, the difference coming only from adding the adjective *historical*. However, in the case of Auschwitz, the simultaneous use of both terms, based on their Polish sense, seems fully justified.

The word *zabytek* (historical monument) derives from *z dawnego bytu* (the reality of the past). In other words, although it concerns the past, when it was created, it was not intended to be a memorial. In Polish, structures intentionally built as memorials are called *pomnik* (monuments), whereas *zabytek* (historical monument) defines buildings, pieces of art, and other objects, some time after they were actually created.

In case of a death camp, a historical monument is what remained after the tragic events of the past. Their shocking symbolism demands a continual presence in the memory of future generations. This symbolism was given material form by, among others, the International Monument to the Victims of the Camp, which was erected on the grounds of the former Auschwitz II – Birkenau camp.

Shortly after the end of World War II, it was accepted that the death camp would be treated as a historical monument, generally within the confines of the barbed wire fences, thus encompassing the entire grounds of Auschwitz I and Auschwitz II – Birkenau. This decision was based on the assumption that conservation care should be extended to important material remains from "the reality of the past"– including the most tragic ones.

The addition of the former Auschwitz grounds, together with preserved buildings and facilities, to UNESCO's World Heritage List, emphasized its significance. The international community accepted the declaration of the Polish government, saying that it would ensure proper protection of this monument, which is of particular importance to humanity. However, during a meeting of international experts debating this issue, there was some controversy because some of the experts preferred that the list include only the achievements of humanity, not examples of its barbarity.

Historical monuments are often called repositories of memory. It seems more accurate, however, to perceive them as stimuli for historical imagination, and particularly of events that deserve a presence in the human conscience. Most historical buildings were silent participants in history. Though old buildings do not speak for themselves, they allow us to read the events of the past. They are documents incorporated in written or spoken testimonies of the past. They are material proofs supplementing and authenticating the accounts and re-constructions of past events. This is the current role played by the remains of Auschwitz; it helps our contemporaries understand the tragic truth, which for them is otherwise "just" history.

Former concentration camps used to be called *historical monuments of martyrdom*. They are distinguished from other historical buildings and settings, which are the source of aesthetic pleasure for their creators. Particular importance ascribed to objects connected with martyrdom has been known for ages and is generally the domain of religion. In Christian culture, the cult of martyred saints, knowledge of their histories, and ample forms of their commemoration, for centuries were inspirations for priests, believers, and artists. Beginning from the fifth century, the crucifix – the central symbol of Christian martyrdom – was omnipresent in Christian societies. It influenced the feelings, moods, and psyches of generations.

Photo: B. Rymaszewski

Auschwitz II-Birkenau. Nature covers up traces of horror.

For thousands of years, humanity has been subjected to all kinds of suffering and mass murder of the innocent, particularly during wars. However, monuments and memorials were built, except for those to martyred saints, only to heroes because nations tend to commemorate fighters, not sufferers. This is why in most of the artistic heritage of the past, one rarely finds nonsacred martyrdom in any of the disciplines of the arts. In centuries past, an artist whose sensibility and feelings were moved by shocking events had few creative outlets as it was difficult to find a patron for such work.

For example, Albrecht Dürer[13] wanted to preserve for future generations the memories of a peasant uprising in Germany. It was impossible, however, to find a founder who would support the artist's idea of commemorating the bloody peasant war of 1525. The only thing the artist could do was to publish a sketch in a manual entitled: *Lessons on Measuring With Compasses and Ruler*. The painter has not defined his political opinions; he simply designed a nonsacred monument of martyrdom, probably for the first time in history, without the unequivocal declaration of support of any of the parties

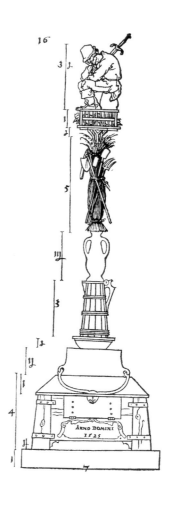

The design of the monument to commemorate the peasants' war in Germany, 1525. Drawing by Albrecht Dürer.

[13] Albrecht Dürer (1471-1528), leading German painter, graphic artist and theoretician of art.

whom he would recognize as particularly worth commemorating. In his sketch of the monument, he placed a peasant in the pose of the Sorrowful Christ pierced with a sword and sitting at the top of a column formed by various peasant tools.

Neither before nor after can we find any other works of arts created with similar intentions, although the glorification of political martyrdom has appeared many times as a theme in poetry or literature. However, in such cases, an author always identified the positive hero. In Polish culture, the example was the personality of Conrad, who suffered for millions, created in a poetic drama by Adam Mickiewicz.[14]

Romantic martyrs, like the ones depicted in earlier times, were heroes by choice. They were solitary, encircled fighters. In the 20th century, countless masses of people were thrown into martyrdom, regardless of their political orientation or attitudes. They were victims of totalitarian systems, of mechanisms created for inflicting violence and destruction; they had almost no chance to resist or fight.

After World War II, a new discipline was created: the science of martyrology. The term derives from two Greek roots: *martys* (witness, martyr) and *–logy* (knowledge). Martyrology emerged when, during the postwar years, large numbers of places and events related to nonreligious martyrdom were brought to public attention. When juxtaposed with the term *monument*, martyrology obliges us to take proper care of credible evidence.

---

[14] The greatest poet of Polish Romanticism, Adam Mickiewicz (1798-1855), in the third part of the poetic drama *"Dziady,"* written after the fall of the November Uprising in 1831, in a scene taking place in prison. The setting was a novelty in world literature, in its expression of a metaphysical belief in the importance of suffering in the name of the Motherland as a means for redemption.

A monument does not have to fulfill the objectives of a document; taking over the role of a symbol, it stimulated the memory with artistic values. It is erected to express feelings, most often connected with political intentions. It receives its material shape from an artist without necessarily keeping the precise fidelity of a historical message. The historical monument, in turn, acts as a witness to the reality of the past.

This difference has not been respected in previous centuries, particularly in the 19th century, when numerous historical buildings were restored. Usually, they were called monuments. The restoration of many buildings was based on shaping them in an historical form based on the artist's imagination, but violating their original shape. This enhanced the expression of several historical monuments, but, at the same time, they were stripped of their historical credibility because the historical message had been altered. Eugene Emmanuel Viollet-le-Duc,[15] prominent French scholar, architect, and conservator, used to justify such an approach. In his *Dictionnaire raisonne de l'architecture francaise du XI-e au XVI-e siecle* (Dictionary of French architecture from the 11th to the 16th century) he wrote: "To restore a historical monument does not mean to preserve, fix, or rebuild it – it means to restore it to the state of integrity, in which it might have never been before."

This opinion is worth remembering. Although expressed not very long ago, it still has many supporters and followers.

---

[15] Eugene Emmanuel Viollet-le-Duc (1814-1879), French architect, conservator, historian and theoretician of architecture. In the 19th century, his imposing professional accomplishments and opinions on the conservation of historical monuments, (most of which were rejected in the 20th century) enjoyed great understanding and support, and had numerous followers in the so-called purist conservation movement, which was based on removing later changes and giving an historical monument uniform shape (usually Gothic).

Unintentionally, it became a warning for some attempts at restoration and conservation, which should not take place in a historical monument and in the complex of a former death camp in particular. It cannot be a place of architectural reconstructions, but solely of preservation and adaptation of as narrow a scope as possible. The latter is obviously inevitable in a view of the present function of the buildings. It creates

Shoes of victims (a museum exhibition at Auschwitz I).

the need to prepare the proper facilities for accommodating several hundred thousand visitors who come every year to the former Auschwitz grounds for any number of reasons. In visiting, they want to see the actual scene of the tragic events, the funeral place for the victims of mass murder, visit real buildings and the machinery of the death factory, and to experience the unquestioned, secular relics of martyrs of the 20th century.

The abundant numbers of visitors must have at least a minimum of infrastructure, which usually accompanies tourist services. This is why it is justifiable to find places around the camp to build car parks, toilets, small bars, post offices, and bookshops. Together with a conference room and cinema

Photo: B. Rymaszewski

Auschwitz I. Roll-call square. Reconstruction of the collective gallows in the background.

room, these services are necessary for the functioning of the museum and must be located in its immediate vicinity, but outside the campgrounds surrounded by barbed wire fences. The storage space for museum exhibits and archives are located in former camp blocks, and most of the offices and workshops necessary for the museum's function were placed in buildings formerly used by the SS. They currently accommodate administration, garages, storage space for equipment, and specialized conservation and craft workshops, which ensure ongoing conservation work for preserving the historical buildings and exhibits.

The need for preserving historical monuments without reconstruction was convincingly justified as early as 1886 by

Auschwitz. Crematorium installations.

Camillo Boito[16] in his book entitled *I nostri vecchi monumenti* (Our historical monuments). Boito compared a historical

---

[16] Camillo Boito (1842-1914), Italian architect, historian of art and conservator, professor of the Brera Academy in Milan. Author of publications of crucial importance for European conservation practice. Among other works, in 1893, he published *Questioni pratiche di belle arti* (Practical aspects of the fine arts).

monument to a book that he prefers to read "with no abbreviations, supplements or changes." These words represent criticism of reconstructing historical buildings or even their elements, after any sort of previous destruction.

At the beginning of the 20th century, several intellectuals (e.g., Prosper Merimee[17], Victor Hugo[18], and Józef Ignacy Kraszewski) formulated a theory of preservation and conservation of historical monuments. According to this theory, the only purpose of such activity should be to conserve the current status of a historical monument and not to permanently reconstruct a structure that has ceased to exist.

In 1903 Aloise Riegl[19] published a paper entitled *Der moderne Denkmalkultus, sein Wesen und seine Entstehung* (Contemporary cult of historical monuments, its essence and genesis), which is still considered by the international community as the current basis for conservation methodology. When Riegl defined the value of historical monuments in his paper, he could not predict the events of Auschwitz. The sources of the cult of historical monuments he presented were obviously addressed to buildings different from the ones found in a death camp; nevertheless, most of the values Riegl defined, like *historical value, documentary value* or *antiquity*, can be applied to it. They are elements of authenticity, which is a prerequisite for recogni-

---

[17] Prosper Merimee (1803-1870), French writer, member of the Academy of France, author of historical fiction; he supported preservation of historical monuments without improving them.

[18] Victor Marie Hugo (1802-1885), French writer, poet and politician. The most eminent theoretician of Romanticism. He criticized the practice of reconstructing historical monuments which, in his opinion, was like trying to turn an aged woman into a young girl.

[19] Aloise Riegl (1858-1905), leading Austrian historian and theoretician of art, recognized as a father of the modern approach to the essence of historical monuments and the basis of their professional preservation and conservation.

zing a building as a historical monument. A copy, as Riegl rightly says, possesses no such meaning.

Considering the conservation approach to Auschwitz, one cannot forget the principle "conserve, not restore." It is an unequivocal rejection of reconstruction.

The only justified exception to this rule is the rebuilding of whole historical cities intentionally destroyed by invaders

Auschwitz II-Birkenau. The International Monument of the Victims of the Death Camp - bronze commemorating plates.

during World War II. Such reconstruction took place in Poland after 1945. Professor Jan Zachwatowicz,[20] wrote:

[20] Jan Zachwatowicz (1900-1976), architect, historian of art, conservator, professor of the Department of Architecture at the University of Warsaw, first Chief Conservator of Poland. He enjoyed great international authority and was particularly devoted to the reconstruction of Polish historical monuments destroyed during World War II. For many years he was chairman of the Council for Conservation of Monuments of Struggle and Martyrdom.

"We cannot agree with destruction of monuments of our culture, and thus we will reconstruct them from their foundations to preserve their form, if not authentic, but at least as precise as it lives in our memory and can be found in archive materials, for future generations." At the same time, he emphasized that the current situation justified conscious suspension of the universal rules of scientific conservation.

Photo: L. Foryciarz

Suitcases of victims (a museum exhibition at Auschwitz I)

More important issues, such as preserving national identity, which was inevitably connected with historical monuments, justified this.

The Nazis decided to destroy precious historical buildings in Poland on the basis of the guidelines from *Mein Kampf*, which explicitly said: "Deprive a nation of the monuments of its past, and within two generations it will cease to be a nation." After the Warsaw Uprising, special German squads systematically demolished the capital of Poland. Hitler's objective was to make it disappear from the map of Europe forever. The Nazis turned Warsaw's historical center in a vast heap of rubble. After the city was liberated, an opinion was sometimes expressed that the Warsaw Old Town should

Auschwitz I. A fragment of the permanent exhibition of children's martyrology.

be left in such condition as a "permanent ruin – a proof of German barbarity." Theoretically, this agreed with the scientific principles of conservation. Leaving the Old Town as a permanent ruin would be an unintentional execution of the plans of the Nazis; nevertheless it would be extremely difficult from a technical point of view.

The authentic heap of rubble would have a symbolic meaning and documentary value, but stripped of architectural forms it would merely be a scrap of the "link, essential for the further development of Polish culture," a precious tool for shaping the mentality of future generations. This assumption gave the moral right to re-create a historical form of the demolished city, whose exceptional importance now comes not from an authentic message from past centuries, but in the materialized will of a majority of the nation to restore "a form of monuments of the past, if not authentic, at least precise."

Attitudes toward Auschwitz, generally humane and patriotic, led to conclusions different from the ones that were the basis for restoration of complexes of historical architecture intentionally destroyed. The current and future meaning of historical monuments of martyrdom is based on their certain authenticity, the value of secular relics containing the power of testimonies and feelings. This is why they should only undergo conservation aimed at preserving the remaining substance and not actions aimed at restoring their previous condition.

The complex of the former Auschwitz has a characteristic spatial structure – a result of its ghastly function. As a whole, it creates a monumental complex connected with the town of Oświęcim and the village of Brzezinka and forms a particular historical landscape. This historical cityscape, so different from others, has particular meaning for the memory of the whole of humanity, but it is not because it would document exceptional creative or technical achievements, such as the Great Wall of China, the pyramids of Egypt or the Gothic cathedrals of France. The exceptional value of Auschwitz comes from the fact that in a sea of evil committed by mankind throughout its entire history, it is distinguished as the most representative, precisely designed instrument of destruction of humanity, a document of tragic events that took place in a century proud of comprehensive progress and universal humanitarian ideas, including human rights.

This area whose surface is 191 hectares (including 171 hectares of Auschwitz II-Birkenau and 20 hectares of Auschwitz I) has been recognized as a historical monument,

Auschwitz II-Birkenau. Interior of brick barrack.

and now it represents the most explicit part of the vast, former camp. During the German occupation, it consisted of several dozen subcamps, numerous industrial plants, mines, fields, and roads, which were the places of torture and death of prisoners. Certainly, it is impossible to preserve the original landscape from the times of murder. In many places, the only reminders of the terrible days are plaques and other artistic forms of commemoration as well as written or recorded accounts. A similar way of commemorating the historical events took place in Warsaw, which was completely destroyed during World War II, and is now entirely rebuilt, modern and growing. However, this has not obliterated the memory that this city was once rendered a heap of rubble, and its every corner was soaked with blood.

Since Auschwitz was liberated, the landscapes and atmosphere of Oświęcim and Brzezinka have changed greatly compared to the time of occupation. This was expected, natural, and necessary. The sky is no longer covered with smoke from chimneys of the crematoria, and nature softens the horrible pictures of the past.

Auschwitz ceased to exist as an active death factory. However, it cannot disappear from human memory. This memory is naturally aided by preserved fragments of camp structures, which inspire the contemplation of the reasons for, history and results of the tragedy that took place here. Here, nothing needs to be added or invented. Everything is tangible and painfully real. The existence of material structures, a vast mechanism for murdering people, should first of all document the unprecedented events and create the respect deserved by the victims. It should lead to deep, honest reflections, free from attitudes, which are the cause of such isolated ideas such as arranging real camp scenes in the actual historical setting. Such suggestions might be justified in film scenes, as those, with the exception of authentic documentary films, usually depict the artists' generally subjective ideas of the concentration camps.

All ideas for constructing realistic scenes of the past on the campgrounds must be categorically rejected. The proposals, like those for placing wax dummies to more suggestively depict participants in the camp tragedy, are mistaken by definition. Realization of such ideas would violate the solemn atmosphere of the place, would mean profanation and lack of respect for the victims. The scenes formed with the use of naturalistic dummies (which is currently practiced at various historical exhibitions, including some museums in the United

Photo: B. Rymaszewski

Auschwitz II-Birkenau. A fragment of the camp fence.

States) in faithfully reconstructed clothes and using authentic tools, surrounded by the buildings which were the actual scene of the past events would only create an illusion of the things that have happened here, but it could not recall a tragic, faithful picture of the past, never mind the feelings associated with it. The obvious truth is that deep feelings, meditation, and reflection can only be evoked by true, real testimonies.

During the five years of the functioning of Auschwitz, many scenes deserving commemoration took place in every corner of the camp – not the only one selected for such an exhibition. Also, it should not be forgotten that in later years, many other events took place at the former camp grounds and though they happened in different situations, they were equally important for the history of this place and left their lasting impression on it. Failing to mention them would be the same as falsifying them.

A procession of victims and torturers disappeared from the space of Auschwitz forever. A horrifying melody of voices died away, and the stench of burned bodies and the sweat of the tortured ones dispersed. The atmosphere of fear and extreme fatigue also disappeared. Smell and hearing cannot currently recognize the original nature of the camp's reality. It is only sight that can recognize it, aided by the conscience of the past events and changes that took place in this historical area and its neighborhood.

During the functioning of Auschwitz II-Birkenau, the area surrounded by barbed wire did not contain a single blade of grass, except for the flowerbeds kept for propaganda reasons. If such grass survived by accident, the feet of thousands of prisoners stamped on it before it began to grow. Terribly hungry prisoners, for whom they were a tempting source of vitamins, immediately picked small plants surviving by miracle.

Today lush green plants grow around. There are some attempts to curb their growth so that they do not dominate and obliterate the remaining camp structures. This does not signal an intention to restore the pre-1945 landscape with clouds of dust and huge areas of mud. The current activity is solely a result of the care for preserving harmony between traces of historical events and changes that inevitably come every year.

Beginning in late January 1945, normal life began to revive in Oświęcim, Brzezinka, and surrounding villages. Many original owners returned to the land, which during the occupation was a closed zone surrounded by the SS posts separating the area where the horrors took place and the neighborhoods inhabited by Poles. The local farms began to operate; new houses, workshops and other village or town facilities were built. They were built also in the areas where prisoners were exploited during the occupation and where many of them died.

These things happened over an area of several thousand hectares, in nearby factories, mines, farm fields or roads. All these places could not remain in the ghastly condition of the occupation years. Important elements connected with the picture of those horrible times remained only in the separate area conserved and cared for by the museum staff. This area is the very core of the camp abyss. This space, though much larger than any other similar commemoration places, is just the most important part of the former camp where a great tragedy took place.

Life obliges us to preserve the places that are important to our history, but also to create the space for normal existence free from the burden of the past. Thus, care was taken to preserve the immediate instrument of crime and the proofs confirming that it took place. It consists of areas where human ashes were deposited and of various camp structures and tools, which are located mainly in the area surrounded by the fence of concrete posts with barbed wire. The conservation care was also extended to sites that were crucial for the history of Auschwitz, like the mass graves of murdered Soviet prisoners of war, the former crematorium No. 1, the railway siding with a building of the State Tobacco Monopoly, the camp admissions building and some of the places used by the SS, like the camp commander's house and guardhouse. The immediate jurisdiction of the State Museum of Auschwitz-Birkenau covered a complex consisting of 154 buildings (56 at Auschwitz I and 98 at Auschwitz II-Birkenau), 300 ruins of barracks, gas chambers and crematoria, thirteen 844-meter--long fences and huge numbers of objects and documents connected with the camp victims, including 2000 kg of hair and 80 m³ of shoes. All those, together with numerous written documents, photographs and accounts of former prisoners draw a picture of the existence of Auschwitz from 1940 to 1945.

Memories of the tragic experience that emanate from this historical monument became a source for artistic inspiration. They resulted in numerous literary, poetic, and musical works, films, paintings, and sculptures. The largest of the sculptures is a monument at the former Auschwitz II-Birkenau grounds. The idea of commemorating the camp victims was present in many parts of society from the first moments after liberation, but it was completed as late as 1967. Over 20 years, the discussions on choosing the most appropriate place and form of the monument were connected with wide-reaching reflections on the future of the former camp grounds and buildings and on their contemporary meaning.

The trials of Nazi war criminals, including the Auschwitz SS-men, which repeatedly took place for many years after the war, confirmed the meaning of the remaining camp buildings and relics as doubtless proof of the crimes committed in this place. This was an extremely important argument for preserving the authenticity of this historical monument to martyrdom.

At the former camp grounds the principle of pure conservation, including very modest adaptations, was waived only very rarely, and fortunately to minimal extent. Such a case was the reconstruction of gallows located at the roll-call square in the main camp (*Stammlager*) or the rebuilding of

Photo: B. Rymaszewski

Auschwitz I. A fragment of the concrete fence.

No. 1 crematorium. This was done a few years after liberation, in the period when a trend toward reconstructing the historical monuments destroyed during the war was dominant in Poland. Also, in those days, many former prisoners, who survived the camp nightmare, called for the display of the instruments of crime to visitors to Auschwitz.

Among the preserved items was an original Nazi plan of a gas chamber and of a crematorium at Auschwitz I. Also, cast iron furnaces and trolleys with which it was originally equipped, remained intact. They were dismantled during the camp's operation when the rooms were converted into an anti-aircraft shelter for the SS-men. Later the crematoria equipment was stored. It was recovered after liberation, and, a few years after the museum was established, the decision was taken to restore them again to the place where they were the cause of such a great death toll. Also, the crematorium's chimney was reconstructed.

In 1957, an international competition for the design of an International Monument to the Victims of Auschwitz II-Birkenau was announced. The participants were clearly requested that the designed installation "should not violate the preserved character of the former camp grounds." Nevertheless, the majority of presented concepts included significant changes to the specific historical landscape. This was also true for the design by Oskar Hansen[21], which was chosen as the best one. It had grand proportions, which, according to the artist, were essential to emphasize the importance of the commemorated tragedy. The artist planned, for example, to build a vast transverse road made of black stone plaques running across the entire Auschwitz II-Birkenau grounds. This was his way to symbolically cross the death camp out. Adopting such a design, however, would lead to destroying extremely important elements of a spatial and structural document, which is an historical monument of martyrdom. Apart from a few blocks, this would lead to the destruction

---

[21] Oskar Hansen (born 1922), architect and professor of the Academy for Fine Arts in Warsaw.

of, among others, fragments of the ramp where selections took place or the ruins of a gas chamber and a crematorium. The jury, who was fascinated with the dynamism of the artistic vision, approved the suggestive design and its artistic value. Professor Jan Zachwatowicz, then the Chief Conservator of Poland, put much effort in preventing the realization of this idea and saving the historical spatial structure of

Auschwitz II-Birkenau. A drawing in one of the prisoners' barracks.

Auschwitz II-Birkenau and numerous important camp relics from destruction.

After a few years of discussion another design, shaped by several authors, was adopted. The memorial was erected without altering the preserved camp structures. Modestly segmented, rough stone blocks look as if they were blended with the surroundings and together with these surroundings they help in deep reflection. There is no attempt to present a story. The emotional expression is left to the largely untouched camp grounds, the preserved buildings and structures, museum exhibitions, and written or spoken accounts. This character is also preserved in over a dozen bronze plaques with inscriptions, including the necessary minimum of words written in the mother tongues of the camp victims.

Museum

The State Museum in Oświęcim, which has functioned since the 1950s, attracts several hundred thousand visitors, making it one of the busiest Polish museums. However, it is rather difficult to reconcile the character of the place with the definition of a museum, as defined by the International Commission of Museums (ICOM) in the 1950s. According to the ICOM, a museum is a permanent, nonprofit institution, in service of society and its development, whose task is to gather, maintain, study, popularize, and exhibit material evidence concerning man and his environment for the purpose of studying, education and pleasure. Of course, the latter part of the prescribed role can by no means be related to the objects connected with martyrdom.

It seems worthwhile to note a partly forgotten ancient definition of a museum, that is: a "residence of Muses." Among the muses, a significant role was to be played by Clio, the patron of history, and Melpomene, who had authority over tragedy.

One of the characteristics of martyrdom sites and museums such as Auschwitz is the ideological unity of their sense and objectives. Nevertheless, contradictions, often requiring compromise, may surface. In other words, preserving historical value requires maintaining the site in its original condition, without introducing any changes. On the other hand, a museum should include exhibition arrangements, which makes it difficult to avoid introducing innovations into the original architecture, in particular, in the interiors.

Avoiding innovation is difficult, even when displaying original exhibits connected with the camp and its victims, such as hair, shoes, and other objects. When the camp was functioning they were stored in conditions different from the requirements of museum exhibitions. During the latter, explanatory descriptions, photographs, charts, diagrams, and show cases are provided. Also special lighting of rooms and exhibits is required.

Currently, in Auschwitz I, in the blocks in which thematic exhibitions are arranged or which are used as museum storerooms, archives, and workshops, the transparency of the camp interiors has been obliterated. Only parts of some selected buildings have had their character preserved. For instance, in the Death Block Number 11, both the prison cells and the room of the supervising SS-men are kept in the condition closely resembling that of the times of war.

Comparing martyrological institutions to open-air museums is entirely erroneous because such museums constitute exhibitions of buildings transferred usually from various other places, set in a specially chosen area, in a new, artificial environment whose arrangement intentionally makes it look old. At the beginning of the 20th century, in the galleries of old art, pseudohistoric interiors were arranged through the use of period interior decoration. That served the purpose of arranging sculptures and pictures in a planned order.

Contemporary museology rejects such practices because they hinder the proper perception of historic works of art. Open-air museums specializing, for example, in folk architecture, former industry or military art still tend to create artificial settings for exhibits. Moreover, some museums attempt to demonstrate live the traditional functioning of the displayed historic facilities, such as windmills and craftsmen's workshops. Participants of such exhibitions are sometimes people clad in costume who know how to use the old technologies. In museums devoted to folk culture, live animals are sometimes also used.

In an old castle, as well as in some ancient city complexes, parades, tournaments, and concerts are held in a proper historical mode. In recent decades, the illusion of travelling in a time machine is additionally enhanced by modern techniques, such as sound and light displays. Such techniques bring history closer to the viewers and also provide pleasure. Thus, we can accept them or even praise the special effects used in many museums, including the Louvre, in Paris. Such performances, however, should not take place in institutions of martyrdom the objective of which is to direct the visitors toward the experiences resulting from contact with the true and direct evidence of human drama and not from artificially created effects.

In the 1970s, the new exhibition elements in the blocks of Auschwitz I, in which the so-called National Exhibitions were arranged, dominated the authentic character of the camp interiors. Those exhibitions were agreed upon by the museum management and prepared by individual national committees belonging to the International Auschwitz Committee. Their members were former prisoners of the camp. That initiative resulted mainly in exhibitions composed of charts. Thematically, they transcended the martyrdom at Auschwitz and focused on the problems of martyrdom and fighting with the Nazis in particular countries.

Despite being national, they actually became exhibitions devoted to particular states not nations. This characteristic is verified in the agreements for two exhibitions concerning German martyrdom, one for East Germany and one for West Germany. The considerably advanced preparations were never finalized, however, once the two German states were united.

Within the series of the national exhibitions, apart from the Polish Exhibition, only the Block of Jewish Martyrdom fully corresponds with the issue described in the title. It is also an

Photo: L. Foryciarz

Auschwitz I. A fragment of the permanent exhibition of Jewish martyrology.

example of the radical adaptation of the interior of a brick camp block to the needs of the artistic concept of the exhibition. The exhibition, which among others makes use of audio-visual media, was arranged in 1978 by Poles, including substantial cooperation with some eminent Jewish specialists from abroad.

Italians, on the other hand, introduced into their national exhibition a totally different manner of presentation. Instead of a narrative exhibition, they created a nonfigurative, artistic composition inspired by the martyrdom of their compatriots. This solution reminds us that beside its testimonial function, Auschwitz also stimulates diverse forms of artistic creation to record the contemporary perception

A fragment of the temporary exhibition entitled "The World of Józef Szajna" which is displayed on the grounds of the former camp to commemorate the 50th anniversary of the liberation of Auschwitz.

of the events that took place there. Such character was evident, for instance, in the temporary art exhibition of Józef Szajna[22], a distinguished Polish artist and a former KL Ausch-

---

[22] Józef Szajna (born in 1922) – a distinguished scenographer, painter and author of theatrical performances with a deep and developed metaphorical artistic setting related to the issue of martyrdom. Also, a professor at the Academy of Fine Arts in Warsaw.

witz prisoner. Held in 1995, in the wooden barracks of the camp laundry, it commemorated the 50th anniversary of the camp's liberation.

In the museum established in the area of Auschwitz, apart from the need for the live narratives of the guides, there still exists and will exist the need for a wider use of audiovisual equipment and other additions.

Photo: L. Foryciarz

Auschwitz I. Italian exhibition.

While applying the newest exhibition methods, however, far-reaching moderation is also indispensable. Usually these methods are used to improve the perception of the ideas presented and to stimulate a deeper experience, but they must not veil the authenticity, which is the supreme value of the museum space.

A Place of Remembrance

In some countries, particularly in Germany, martyrdom museums are officially referred to as Places of Remembrance. This results from their wide use for political manifestations and religious practices. Not long ago, the State Museum Auschwitz-Birkenau in Oświęcim also started to add "a Place of Remembrance" to its official name. After World War II, in Poland such a name was given to many thousands and thousand of places connected with martyrdom and with the struggle for liberty.

Nowadays, in most of these places, there are monuments of various sizes or commemorative plaques. Poles also refer to war and army cemeteries or single graves, battlefields, and former prisons and camps as Places of Remembrance. A similar role is played by several thousand Chambers of Remembrance furnished mostly at schools, as well as by several dozen museums, which house exhibitions concerning that subject. About a dozen are established in some parts of the former Nazi camps or prison buildings. At present, beside the exhibitions and the necessary museum base, they also possess properly furnished halls where homage can be paid to those who died in battles or were murdered.

In Poland, as well as in other countries, Places of Remembrance are identified with the parts of individual buildings or whole complexes, which once functioned as a significant tool of the mass murder machine. The edifice in Aleja Szucha in Warsaw is one such example. In the years of the German occupation, it was a Gestapo headquarters and a place of torture. At present, as before the war, the building is the seat of the Ministry of Education.

The character of a museum and a Place of Remembrance is limited only to a small part – some of the cellars that in the past functioned as a Gestapo prison. Their appearance is maintained in such a way as to sustain the look of the

The wall in the Memorial Site; the former Gestapo prison at Szucha Avenue in Warsaw.

occupation period. Among others, the inscriptions that the prisoners scratched on the walls with their own fingers have been preserved in one of the cells. One of these inscriptions, evoking the drama of those days, reads as follows: "It is easy to talk about Poland, it is more difficult to work for it, even more difficult to die for it, but to suffer for it is the most difficult." The documentary

The Memorial Site at Szucha Avenue in Warsaw.

and emotional significance of these pieces of plaster has made conservation necessary. Increasing the legibility would violate the authenticity of the sentence. That is why it is repeated in a magnified form in the museum hall, on the main wall at which flowers are put and candles are lit in this Place of Remembrance.

Photo: B. Rymaszewski

A cell of the Gestapo prison at Szucha Avenue in Warsaw.

The new emotional values of particular elements of the martyrdom monuments are sometimes conceived as a result of the events related to paying homage to the victims. The evidence of this is, for instance, an old tree functioning as a natural monument; this tree has been preserved in Warsaw in front of the Pawiak ruins. During the German occupation, the place was a Gestapo prison. On the dry trunk, conserved several years ago, hang numerous obituaries. They have been placed there since the first moments after the liberation to commemorate those who were tortured to death by the Nazis. Before abandoning the building, the torturers managed to blow it up. In the 1960s, the ruins, the preserved cellars and the fragments of the ground-floor walls were converted after

Photo: B. Rymaszewski

The building of the Ministry of Education during the II World War the Gestapo Headquarters.

conservation to a martyrdom museum: a Place of Remembrance.

Both these examples from Warsaw show that combining the museum function with the concern for preserving the authentic character of the historical message and with the natural need to venerate the memory of the victims is neither easy nor without

The Monument; the tree in front of the former Gestapo prison, in Warsaw.

conflict. On the one hand, there are attempts to introduce artistic arrangements, which contribute to the evoking of deeper feelings and help to form an emotional attitude toward commemoration. On the other hand, however, there is full awareness of the fact that only historic areas and objects left in their original condition can constitute a reliable testimony and a source of authentic, not falsified, emotions.

Photo: B. Rymaszewski

The Museum - the Memorial Site in the ruins of the demolished prison at Pawiak, in Warsaw.

The dilemmas concerning the two mutually contrasted tendencies – the desire to preserve the authentic things and the tendency to introduce arrangement elements – have also manifested themselves since the 1950s. They are partly illustrated by some of the examples presented. So far the contrasted ideas have been accurately reconciled.

Besides the focused activities undertaken by a group of experts, which may influence the historical message of the camp complex, there also took place some spontaneous processes that were difficult to manage. Lighting candles, the placing of flowers, stones, school badges, flags and scarves are the most frequent, natural forms of paying homage to the victims at Places of Remembrance. However, the concern over control of the excessive filling of historical spaces imposes the requirement to remove those icons of memory and above all to give a uniform framework to these practices and to designate special places for them.

Consequently, as in the case of cemeteries and monuments, also in the museums that are Places of Remembrance, wreaths and bunches of flowers are only allowed to lie there only for a relatively short time because of their natural fading. For this reason, numerous initiatives have been undertaken in the former camp, aimed at installing permanent memorial plaques and signs and introducing various artistic forms dedicated to particular groups of people or even to individuals. This, of course, requires discipline, limitations, and selection. Each particular decision should be based on an analysis to what extent each subsequent motif was significant in the history of Auschwitz and whether it justifies even a minor change in the original condition of the former camp. Without such analyses and limitations, the little cell in which father Maksymilian Kolbe was kept after he had been condemned to death by starvation, would, for instance, quickly lose its authentic character.

It is only natural that celebrations and religious practices of various religious denominations take place in Places of Remembrance. In Auschwitz, sometimes several thousand people participate in them. This requires preparations as well as some special provisional installations, which guarantee efficient organisation and protect the historic places from possible damage.

Continuing Reflections of Auschwitz

In spite of destruction and the passing years, the equipment and buildings preserved in Auschwitz still affect the visitors emotionally. The present landscape of the former death camp comes into close contact with normal, contemporary housing. Nevertheless, it evokes a strong connection to the tragic past. The tragedy must not be forgotten, but the burden of history should not suppress the environment forever. It may not loom over the everyday life of the inhabitants of the town and its neighborhood. They have inalienable rights to feel joy, to live quiet lives, and to satisfy their normal vital needs.

Acknowledging the absolute necessity to respect and maintain all the significant testimonies of the past, we should not fear that they might paralyze modern development. The key to a proper reconciliation of the memory of the tragic past and an optimistic future lies in the accurate perception and proper protection of the most important places devoted to contemplation of the past. At the same time, an area free of gloom should be demarcated because it is indispensable for the dynamic and normal character of contemporary life.

During the years of World War II, the Nazi genocide machine encompassing a considerable part of Europe was particularly severe in Poland. It does not mean, however,

Auschwitz II-Birkenau. Disintegrating concrete posts of the inner fence.

that in preserving the complete truth of those murky times, and in passing it down to subsequent generations, it is necessary to maintain all the elements of the landscape in which those tragic events took place.

Saving from oblivion the places, buildings, and objects connected with history requires a proper selection of those elements that should be left intact because of their character of authentic documents. One of the effective approaches toward such choices derives from historical studies based on the solutions included in site planning and in urban development plans. In the case of Auschwitz, this involves local plans made for the town of Oświęcim and the villages of Brzezinka, Pławy, and Harmęże. These plans have to take into account the decisions of the Voivodeship Conservator of Monuments concerning the buildings and areas that are under the conservator's protection. The conservator also controls the neighborhood connected with the protected historic sites.

According to Polish law the local urban plans have to be made in cooperation with specialist organs of administration (including the Voivodeship Conservator of Monuments) and, then, after canvassing the opinions of the population, they have to be approved by local self-governments. Every few years, the plans are modified and approved again, which guarantees improvement in the processes of urban development. Some special values, for example, connected with martyrdom places, are absolutely respected as permanent and sacred elements. Such plans belong to local jurisdiction, and, in fact, they are decisive as far as the character, form, and function of buildings, as well as the development forms of the whole entities, are concerned.

Auschwitz II-Birkenau. Time destroys the ominous fence.

The former mutual relationships of the death camp and the area of several thousand hectares situated in the zone of SS interests, have been replaced in some way by the present relationship and dependence on the neighbourhood or even entirely by the nearest agglomeration. Today, the former Auschwitz (i.e., within the border of the camps proper) is a

Place of Remembrance, a museum, and a large cemetery, which together with the existing buildings has been entered into the registry of historic sites as a part of the urban complex of the town of Oświęcim and of the community of Brzezinka. This authorizes the conservation institutions to undertake proper practical activities as well as to exert control, the objective of which is to preserve the authentic character

Photo: B. Rymaszewski

Auschwitz II-Birkenau. The ruins of the gas chambers and crematorium V.

of the place. Its neighborhood is also to be managed in such a way that it interferes neither with its historic nor contemporary part.

The statutory purview of the Voivodship Conservator of Monuments and Chief Conservator of Monuments concerns also the protection of the spatial layout and the buildings, while the statutory purview of the director of the State Museum Auschwitz-Birkenau in Oświęcim, involves the protection of the movable parts of the collection. The supervision of all these elements is vested in the Minister of Culture.

At present, the area of the former Auschwitz I and Auschwitz II-Birkenau camps is surrounded by a 100-meter wide protection zone authorized by law. This zone is mostly of administrative significance; for example, it is forbidden to organize there any manifestations or mass gatherings without a permit. However, it has little influence on the layout, which neither violates the documentary or emotional integrity of the camp.

Urban planning that takes into account the protection and the proper use of the significance of Auschwitz has to be based on conservation guidelines, which should, in turn, be based on historical knowledge. Such guidelines take into account contemporary needs and efforts to preserve the value of the historic places of martyrdom. Such plans for Oświęcim and Brzezinka, commissioned by the Foundation for Memory of the Auschwitz-Birkenau Death Camp Victims, have already been drawn up. They suggest that preserving the essential message of the former Auschwitz does not require inhibiting change in the area surrounding Oświęcim.

In other words, prisoners suffered in thousands of places and buildings, such as factories, warehouses, arable fields, or along communication lines. The latter performed and still perform their normal functions, although they once were part of a dramatic death route for almost one and a half million people. Memory cannot focus on identifying currently used railway tracks with particular historic places of martyrdom. In the same way, it is not possible to give a museum-like character to all the sites which witnessed the tragedy. Yet, it is necessary to make sure that there is no clash between their present use and their former function.

Thus, for example, entertainment facilities or discos cannot be situated in the buildings where people used to be killed. However, without any major complications, it is possible to use them for purposes that do not profane the traces of martyrdom. In order to prevent misunderstandings and

Photo: B. Rymaszewski

A housing estate (World War II residential blocks for women prisoners, clothes workshops, SS quarters) near Auschwitz I.

mistakes, all major martyrdom places are marked with appropriate plaques containing information about the events of the occupation period and the witnesses to those events.

The protection of historic complexes does not consist of artificial isolation of strictly protected areas, separated from other places. Instead solutions involve entire urban and regional entities. In this way, development and modernization are not impeded; instead they incorporate harmoniously the values rooted in these places. In the case of Oświęcim, this means putting forward adequate proposals concerning the spatial layout and development, not just for some parts of individual towns or villages but for the entire area. It has to be done in such a way that the development does not efface the documentary elements.

Parallel to the changes taking place in the town of Oświęcim, the architectural landscape surrounding Auschwitz has undergone considerable transformation. This is a natural phenomenon, similar to the changes within the groundcover. However, it should not interfere with the mission of the museum: to pass down to future generations the real picture of the death camp. This task has absolutely to be kept in the forefront while making any development plans.

As far as martyrdom complexes are concerned, the requirement to protect the view of the historic sites and from the historic sites has no literal reference or justification. In conservation practice, it is usually applied to historic castles and old town districts. In the case of Auschwitz, the idea is not to preserve the values of architecture or spatial arrangement because of their aesthetic significance, but to preserve the documentation. Its role and quality of transparency will not sustain any harm, if such contemporary facilities as parking lots, lavatories, vending stalls with publications, flowers, candles, alcohol-free drinks and basic meals–things necessary for the museum visitors–are situated within the range of vision (which is, of course, much more than the strictly observed 100-metre zone). However, the new architectural and other elements introduced into the area of visual contact with the camp buildings should be modest and should not have aggressive shapes or gaudy colors.

Essential for maintaining the present functions designated for Auschwitz is the proper design of the road system for the whole urban area, including the nearest towns and villages. This also concerns the proper distribution of services, such as hotels and catering, as well as all other services

Auschwitz II-Birkenau. The gate closing the passage to the unloading ramp, gas chambers and crematoria IV and V.

constituting a part of the urban infrastructure necessary for tourists.

The architectural designs for the towns and villages, in which the former camp buildings and equipment are situated, should ensure that they are not combined as part of one arrangement with the new elements of the contemporary, functioning town and the housing estates surrounding it. Even in places located a long distance from the camp there should appear no skyscrapers because their shapes are too conspicuous, and some of the camp buildings would be visible from their windows.

In the panorama of the camp, its fence is a symbolic and exceptionally impressive element. In Auschwitz I, it consists of a double row of concrete poles with lamps and electric insulators, to which barbed wire is fixed, and in Auschwitz II-Birkenau, of a single row. When the camp was functioning, there was high voltage in the wire. Together with the densely situated watchtowers, where the SS-men kept guard equipped with machine guns and reflectors, the fence formed a closed circuit, which in Oświęcim and in Brzezinka, was very hard to overcome. The inner sectors and parts of the camp were separated by similar single fences, only without the watchtowers. Apart from that, in Auschwitz I, there was also a fence of concrete panels shading the inside of the camp.

In January 1945, the voltage in the fence was cut off. Since that moment, a very intensive corrosion process of the barbed wires began. Beforehand they were naturally protected by the electric current. Without that protection, exposed to atmospheric phenomena, they soon started to crumble, and had to be exchanged for new ones with the same tangle. It was done in order to maintain the visual character of the camp enclosure and also for practical reasons, namely to keep people from entering the museum unobserved.

As the years passed, the process of physical and chemical destruction affected not only the metal elements but also those made of reinforced concrete. Doubtless, according to the Nazi calculations, the death camp was to fulfill its murderous function within a dozen years or so at most and then would disappear from the surface of the earth. That is why an economical technology was adopted while designing it. It consisted of using poor quality materials, for example, for the poles of the fence. It may also be that the prisoners employed for producing them contributed to some minor extent to the lowering of their quality.

Photo: B. Rymaszewski

Auschwitz II-Birkenau. Inner road.

One way or another, over the passing years, nature has caused considerable damage to the concrete poles, which sometimes take unusual shapes and resemble artistic arrangements with a dramatic message. The idea of maintaining the destroyed fence in its present form finds support in some vital arguments, pointing to the authentic character of these elements and to their symbolic, almost artistic expression. That is why it seems right that the conservation of the poles is undertaken, although it would be easier and cheaper to exchange them for new ones. For practical and financial reasons, however, it is acceptable to introduce some visible complement or even to exchange some of the poles entirely. Such a need results from the requirement to maintain the external fence in good condition.

The general conservation activities within the historic complex of Auschwitz (belonging to the museum) are based on the principle of conserving its existing condition. The justified divergences from that principle are the adaptations connected with the present function. For instance, in order to guarantee the proper temperature and humidity necessary to maintain such a large number of objects and documents connected with the victims, it was necessary to install air-conditioning. The system was introduced inside the brick blocks in former Auschwitz I, which house exhibitions, museum storage-rooms, and archives. A similar idea underlies the interior transformations that are carried out as well as the introduction of completely new installations into the building that during the period of occupation belonged to the complex used for admitting the prisoners into the camp. It is situated not far from the entrance to Auschwitz I, and at present it is being converted into the museum's conservation workshops.

The building of the camp bathhouse in Auschwitz II-Birkenau, after it is refurbished, will house the exhibitions for which so far there has been no room in this area. At the same time, the whole original equipment preserved in this building will be maintained and exposed.

The conservation activities carried out in several hundred individual roofed buildings or ruins, which have survived in the area of Auschwitz I and Auschwitz II-Birkenau have been dictated not just by their condition, but primarily by the roles the given objects played within the death factory. Although in the process of documenting and exposing its mechanisms, all the gears are important, the

Photo: B. Rymaszewski

Auschwitz II-Birkenau. Purifiers.

distribution of their documentary and emotional value is still not even.

For this reason, in the activities aimed at maintaining the physical existence of the preserved buildings, their fragments and the equipment used in the camp, pure conservation is applied to the objects of special significance, for example, to the gas chambers and crematoria ruins. A particular emphasis is put on maintaining their authentic substance. Common repairs, on the other hand, are justified in the case of such objects as the huge sewage-treatment plants situated in Auschwitz II-Birkenau. Replacing even large parts of their walls is acceptable, provided that such are the technical requirements because these facilities were not a direct tool of martyrdom.

The justification for the diversification of the conservation methods as applied to individual objects is implied by their direct connection with mass death. The special character of secular relics, similar to that which is rightly attributed to the victim's hair and personal belongings, should be sought also in many buildings in the camp. Block 11, as well as the Death Wall situated in its vicinity, certainly has such significance. So does the ramp where selections would take place. Also most of the prisoner's blocks and barracks have the emotional value that distinguishes them from the warehouses, workshops, kitchens, potato cellars or SS-men's buildings.

In general, there were three types of buildings in which prisoners were kept in Auschwitz:

1. two-story brick buildings called blocks, situated in the complex of the former army barracks, built during World War I (to some of them, extra stories had already been added during the existence of the camp)
2. one-story barracks built since 1941 on the spot of the former village of Brzezinka, mostly from the material obtained after the demolition of the houses belonging to the evicted inhabitants
3. wooden barracks designed as army stables and passed over to the camp by the Wehrmacht. While they were being put together in Brzezinka, some minor impro-

vements were introduced; among others, brick chimneys were built inside them. These types of buildings were also used for warehouses, toilets, washing rooms, and so on. While almost all the buildings in Auschwitz I have survived until today, in Auschwitz II-Birkenau, only 98 out of 300 have survived. Thirty wooden barracks were burnt by the SS-men just before the liberation of the camp. In this way, they

Photo: B. Rymaszewski

Auschwitz II-Birkenau. Chimneys; the remains of the barracks

were trying to destroy the things and clothes stolen from the victims and stored there because these artifacts testified to the crimes. As it has already been mentioned, about 200 buildings were dismantled after the war.

A forest of chimneys standing free against the background of the fence with watchtowers has become a part of the contemporary landscape of the camp situated in Brzezinka. They are strengthened by a core of reinforced concrete introduced into the smoke ducts, which protects them from collapsing due to gusting wind. In order to make the original location of the destroyed barracks clear, their existing foundations are repaired, and the plants overgrowing them are removed.

Auschwitz II-Birkenau. A brick barracks in danger of collapsing under the weight of the rafter framing.

In the preserved wooden barracks, the conservation consists of exchanging the destroyed wooden elements only to the most limited extent. The strengthening dictated by technical necessity is introduced in such a way that the time of the repair is evident. This is a binding principle as far as all alteration and refurbishment works in the camp area are concerned.

Such, for instance, is the case of the necessary constructions strengthening the brick barracks in Auschwitz II-Birkenau. For economic reasons, very thin brick walls were built originally; after some years, however, they could no longer support the rafter framing and covering of the roof, and they started leaning. Technically, the most appropriate thing to do would be to thicken the walls. This, however, is not

Photo: B. Rymaszewski

Auschwitz II-Birkenau. Barracks and chimneys.

done because then the original effect of the economical building manner would be lost. Thus the pressure of the roof is translated onto a new steel framework inside the buildings, on which the date of its construction is marked.

No exhibitions of any kind are held inside either the brick or the wooden barracks preserved in Auschwitz II-Birkenau.

The buildings have survived for more than 50 years, and their furnishing still consists of the prisoners' wooden-board beds. Their condition resembles the original, going back to the time when the last prisoners left them. In Auschwitz I, inside most of the blocks some changes have taken place in the past 50 years. During that time, they were being adapted to serve the museum needs. Only in some limited areas has the reserve character of the interiors been maintained. This, for instance, concerns Block 11 – the Death Block, where, among others, the last inscriptions scratched on the plasters by the prisoners awaiting execution have been preserved.

The material heritage of Auschwitz consists of the ashes of the murdered people as well as of the buildings and the camp furnishings, the written documents and drawings of the prisoners, the photographs and countless personal belongings, clothes, and hair of the victims. All these things are under the care of the museum staff, together with the works of art thematically connected with the camp, the majority of which were already created after the liberation. Most of these things have either already undergone some conservation, or their conservation will be taking place in the immediate future. The difficulties that arise at this point are connected not only with the necessity to obtain considerable financial means for that purpose, but also with the need to choose the proper approach, one that is both methodologically and technically complicated.

First, this means overcoming the barriers connected with introducing processes not used so far in the conservation of monuments. Second, it requires concluding the complex analyses as a result of which unambiguous answers have to be provided to difficult questions. The major question concerns the extent of our intervention during the renovating and strengthening activities. Yet by their very nature, they have to violate in some way the authenticity of the treated objects. The best illustration of this dilemma is the example of the hair.

Besides the destructive activity of bacteria and the tendency of hair to crumble, it is also subject to losing its original color – the hair has turned grey. The present state of knowledge allows us both to stop the destruction process and to restore

Auschwitz I- In the foreground, a watch-tower and the camp admission building, in the background.

the lost colours, which could testify, for instance, that the murdered people were of different ages. Nevertheless, we have to take into account the fact that the victims' shaven hair still continues to be a biologically active particle of the people whose lives were taken away. This fact obliges us to refrain from artificial regeneration and makes us limit ourselves only to preservative activities. A separate issue is answering the question if and how we can exhibit the hair and what means should be used to stop the processes of its gradual decay.

The tragic heritage of Auschwitz has become an unprecedented historic monument, symbol, museum and a Place of Remembrance, situated in the neighborhood of contemporary and normally inhabited areas. It constitutes a startling docu-

Auschwitz II-Birkenau.

ment that evokes an intensive reflection of the tragic events of the past. As a warning for mankind it has to last for centuries. However, it requires constant and specialized care as well as restrained adaptations. For the sake of faithful memory, everything that remains here should be genuine, without any contemporary reconstruction and correction.

Epilogue

From a methodological and technical point of view, maintaining the adequate technical condition as well as preserving the authenticity of the former death camp, its buildings, furnishings, and objects connected with the victims of Auschwitz, is a very difficult task. Its manifold functions, vast area, diversity of the collected objects, testimonies and documents require some innovative activities. In spite of the wide range of constant conservation works conducted in this area by the museum from the very moment it was established, the passing of time brings about the growing danger that many essential elements of this vast and unique historic complex may be destroyed.

In recent years much has been done to prevent that thanks to the involvement of the governments and societies of many countries. However, what has been completed is the fulfilment of just a tiny part of the large-scale tasks because conservation is a continuous process that cannot be interrupted. That is why constant efforts are made to obtain financial support from this country and from abroad in order to continue the conservation project. Such help is necessary for preserving the material remnants of the largest death factory on the Earth, which functioned in the 20th century in the heart of Europe.

Taking care of the heritage of Auschwitz is a moral obligation of the Polish and international communities. It is also necessary to think of the present inhabitants of Oświę-cim and its surroundings, who were so painfully affected by the Nazi crimes. They have to be guaranteed the right to live normal lives in the land of their forefathers without the heavy burden of the past. Living next to the former death factory is by no means easy, and it must create a considerable psychological burden. Yet history cannot be deleted, and common sense suggests a wise compromise. Thus, all people who are strongly rooted in the contemporary time but who are capable of respecting the past deserve appreciation. This Place of Remembrance, so important in the history of mankind, calls for the respect and care of generations.

Bibliography

Auschwitz 1940-1945. The Key Issues in the History of the Camp. ["Auschwitz 1940-1945. Węzłowe zagadnienia z dziejów obozu"]. A collective work. Editors: Wacław Długoborski and Franciszek Piper. Volume I – *Establishment and Organisation*; Volume II – *Prisoners – Life and Work*; Volume III – *Mass Death*; Volume IV – *Resistance Movement*; Volume V – *Epilogue*; Published by the State Museum in Oświęcim, 1995.

Czech, Danuta, *The Almanac of Events in KL Auschwitz.* ["Kalendarz Wydarzeń w KL Auschwitz"]. Published by the State Museum in Oświęcim, 1992.

Czerner, Olgierd, *Of the Authenticity Value of Historic Monuments* ["O wartości autentyzmu w zabytkach"]. In "Ochrona Zabytków," No. 3, 1974.

Garliński, Józef. *Fighting Oświęcim.* ["Oświęcim walczący"]. London. Published by Odnowa, 1974.

Piper, Franciszek. *How Many People Lost Their Lives in KL Auschwitz. The Number of Victims in the Light of the Sources and Research of 1945-1990.* ["Ilu ludzi zginęło w KL Auschwitz]. Liczba ofiar w świetle źródeł i badań 1945-1990."]. Published by the State Museum in Oświęcim, 1992.

Madajczyk, Czesław, *The Policy of the Third Reich in Occupied Poland.* ["Polityka III Rzeszy w okupowanej Polsce"]. Published by PWN, Warsaw, 1970.

Małachowicz, Edmund, *The Protection of the Culture Environment.* ["Ochrona środowiska kulturowego"]. 2 volumes; Published by PWN, Warsaw, 1988.

Nazi Death Camps in the Territories of Poland, 1939-1945. ["Obozy hitlerowskie na ziemiach polskich 1939-1945"]. A collective work. Editor: Czesław Pilichowski. Published by PWN, Warsaw, 1979.

Rawecki, Marek, *The Protection Zone.* ["Strefa ochrony"]. In "Pro Memoria," No. 2, 1995.

Rawecki, Jadwiga, & Rawecki, Marek; *The Museum Protection Zone and a Trade Centre*. ["Strefa ochronna Muzeum a centrum handlowe"]. In "Pro Memoria," No. 5, 1996.

Rawecki, Jadwiga, & Rawecki, Marek; *Memory Antinomies*. ["Antynomie pamięci"]. In "Pro Memoria," No. 7, 1997.

Rymaszewski, Bohdan, *The Key Issues of Historic Monuments Protection in Poland*. ["Klucze ochrony zabytków w Polsce"], Published by the Documentation Centre of Historic Monuments, Warsaw, 1992.

Rymaszewski, Bohdan, *Divagations on Preserving the Memory of KL Auschwitz-Birkenau*. ["Rozważania o zachowaniu pamięci o KL Auschwitz-Birkenau"]. In *Pomerania, Poland, Europe. Studies and Materials to the 19th - and 20th-Century History*. ["Pomorze, Polska, Europa. Studia i materiały z dziejów XIX i XX wieku]. Toruń, 1995.

Rymaszewski, Bohdan, *The Former KL Auschwitz-Birkenau – the State Museum Auschwitz-Birkenau*. ["Byłe KL Auschwitz – Birkenau – Państwowe Muzeum Oświęcim-Brzezinka"]. In "Muzealnictwo," No. 37, 1995.

Rymaszewski, Bohdan, *They Are Also Testimonies of the 20th Century*. ["To też są świadectwa XX wieku"]. In "Pro Memoria," No. 3, 1995.

Ryszka, Franciszek, *The Country in the State of Emergency. On the State and Law System of the Third Reich*. ["Państwo stanu wyjątkowego. Rzecz o systemie państwa i praw Trzeciej Rzeszy"]. Ossolineum, Wrocław-Warsaw-Gdańsk-Łódź-Cracow, 1985.

Smoleń, Kazimierz, *Auschwitz 1940-1945*. ["Oświęcim 1940-1945"]. Published by the State Museum in Oświęcim, 1961.

Smoleń, Kazimierz, & Świebocka, Teresa, in cooperation with Renata Bogusławska-Świebocka, *Auschwitz – a Crime of Genocide*. ["Auschwitz – zbrodnia przeciwko ludzkości"]. Warsaw, 1990.

Szymańska, Irena, *The Monument of Martyrdom of the Polish Nation and Other Nations*. ["Pomnik Męczeństwa narodu Polskiego i innych Narodów"]. In *The Bulletin of the Society for the Care of Auschwitz*, No. 16.

Wysocki Wiesław, Jan, *Captain Pilecki*. ["Rotmistrz Pilecki"]. Gryf Publishing House, Warsaw, 1993.

Zachwatowicz, Jan, *The Program and Principles of Conservation of Historic Monuments*. ["Program i zasady konserwacji zabytków"]. In *The Bulletin of History of Art and Culture*, No. 1/2, 1946.